A God Experience
In the Light

A transcendent experience
of the spirit

Sandy Briggs

A God Experience In the Light
Copyright © 2015 by Sandy Briggs

Some names have been changed to protect their privacy.

Scripture quotations taken from the New English Bible,
copyright © Cambridge University Press and Oxford
University Press 1961, 1970. All rights reserved.

Photo by: www.hqwallbase.com

ISBN-978-1-4951-5181-1

Library of Congress Control Number: 2015904264

Printed in the United States of America

Dedication

To God be the Glory

Table of Contents

About the Author

In her incredible life journey, Sandy discovers new insights about life and the afterlife through empirical spiritual experiences. Meeting God in the Light and receiving information through divine communication opened her eyes to a new perspective of life itself. She was given a glimpse into life in the spirit world that she had never conceived in the past.

This book is intended on taking the reader on a journey to discover the spiritual realm.

Prior to her near-death-like and other spiritual experiences, Sandy had been heavily involved with church and children's activities. She was a Sunday School teacher, Youth Leader and director of Christmas and Easter Pageants. She worked for the school system as a payroll clerk, SIMS operator and substitute teacher.

Sandy is currently a member and forum administrator for ACISTE (American Center for the Integration of Spiritually Transformative Experiences) and NDE-Space. She is also a member of IANDS (International Association for Near-Death Studies, Inc.), NHNE (NewHeavenNewEarth) and assists the TRIAD IANDS Support Group. She is married with two grown children and one grandchild.

About the Book

A God Experience In the Light is my personal experiences of spiritual transformation through: Out-of-Body, Near-death, divine visions, revelations of life beyond Earth, conjoined veridical pre-birth memories, and other spiritual aberrations.

I was drowning in the violent storms of life and became stuck in deep depression at the age of 23. I agonized over why life was so cruel and unfair, eventually losing all hope and desperately prayed for God to end my life.

Expecting death, never would I imagine that my life would take on a renewed awakening of spiritual transformation. I experienced an Out-of-Body / Near-Death-Like, spiritual journey into the Light. To my surprise, my life did not end. I found myself in another realm in the presence of God in Glory! My life was renewed with meaning and purpose and I was sent back to share my testimony of life beyond.

One
The Setting - Introduction

I grew up in a middle-class suburban community south of Pittsburgh, Pennsylvania. Throughout my life, I've experienced a number of different forms of spiritual events which propelled me to search for understanding of things not seen by all people. I've always pondered internally about things which I soon discovered were considered beyond the norm of conventional beliefs. Because I had experienced spiritual things and had no one to share them with as a child, I felt out of place and always in search of something. I was a seeker of truth. But when I consider some things which I personally witnessed and compare them with contradictory ideas which are generally believed by the general consensus, I often feel that our world forces us to conform to its way of thinking, but at the expense of denying the truth. This does not rest well within my soul.

I am hoping that my testimony and life experiences in connection with the spirit will help other people to expand and embrace more of their spiritual side of existence. There are so many testimonies from other people as well as in various religious doctrines which support my experiences, and yet the generally held beliefs of most people often reject them. By my earnest ambition to stick with the spiritual discoveries I had uncovered, I traveled the path to seek for more understanding of spiritual things beyond our world. I've had an amazing life journey but I also endured many turbulent bouts of depression before finding what I did. This is how it all began . . .

Around the age of eleven or twelve, I began contemplating about what characteristics I'm looking for in my future husband. At this point in my life I hadn't thought about dating yet, but I saw how difficult marriage can be by observing other people. I wanted to think this out logically before I start to date. I wanted to fare better than those who married for love and have nothing to fall back on when their feelings fade, then divorce.

The reason I'm sharing this is because it all ties into my future where this all comes into play and leads me on a winding path of self-discovery with spiritual ties, eventually taking me on a spiritual journey into Heaven and back. I learned that there's more to life than this physical world and it's connected to an eternal journey.

As I contemplated about my possible future, I first focused on my personal qualities and I recognized some areas where I felt that I lacked in perfection. Then I focused on those areas that I admired in others and considered those areas as the half of me that was missing. I figured if I could find a man who had those qualities then perhaps he would fill in the half I was missing and we'd be whole as a marriage. I was hopeful that I would find happiness and fulfillment.

1) I recognized that I had difficulty remembering dates and events in history but I saw

the benefit for my future children if they had a parent who naturally retained information about world affairs and history. I wanted my children to appreciate and embrace different cultures and different ethnicities around the world.

2) I recognized that I lacked confidence to speak up in public. I was meek and wanted to avoid confrontation, but if the need for change came about, especially when there were problems, could I stand up for the cause? I wanted a husband who had confidence and wasn't afraid to speak up in public.

3) I wanted to learn more about God, so I wanted a husband who loved God and was brought up in the church. I wanted him to be a leader because I was more of a follower.

4) In relation to the above, I didn't want my husband to be materialistic, greedy or to be focused on fame, fortune or power. I just wanted a simple middle-class family without the high society egos.

5) I didn't want a husband who was vein or arrogant. I wanted him to be average looking, strong, caring and sensitive.

6) I didn't want my husband to smoke, do drugs or be an alcoholic. I wanted to start off on the best foundation without dealing with any addictions.

Overall, I wanted to live a life that felt right, moral and pleasing to God. I set my mind to remember my list and should I find a man who fit these qualifications, I would marry him. Inadvertently, I was setting up my future lessons from the perspective of an innocent, naive point of view. Not long after this time of reflecting, I was soon to explore this path.

When I turned thirteen, I had my first encounter with a boy of interest during summer vacation break from school. Although I wasn't thinking about dating yet, this boy showed me special attention and eventually gave me my first romantic kiss. From that day forward, something changed within me and my heart melted in his presence. Although we never went out on a date, we saw each other often throughout the summer months, but many people were always nearby.

Each time we met, my heart grew fonder with passion and he was always on my mind. I couldn't wait to see him and to feel his arms around me again. I was head over heals in love with him, waiting in anticipation for him to ask me for a date.

When summer vacation ended and I started back to Junior High, I continued to carry thoughts of him in my heart throughout the day. Weeks turned into months but we never saw each other. I wondered why he never called me and never asked me out on a date. It was evident every time we saw each other during the summer months that he was attracted to me. His gentle caresses and passionate kisses drew me in.

Why did he suddenly stop after school started back up? I kept thinking and analyzing in my mind what could be preventing him from contacting me. He was four years older than me and at my age of 13, that made a big difference.

Could this be the reason? But then, my young age didn't stop him from secretly kissing me during the few precious brief moments we escaped an audience. Why would he give me so much attention and hold me in his arms, kissing me with such passion and then without warning, just break it off?

I had no closure and was consumed with emotional conflict. I felt an intense hole in my heart. It was so easy and gentle to open my heart to his love, but so cruel and unbearable to suddenly have him out of my life. There was nothing I could do but feel the sting of rejection. How could he hurt me like that? My very first experience with love and it felt like a knife.

With each passing month, the hole in my heart grew deeper and wider. It took me five years to make myself move on from the strong hold he had over my heart. During those five years, I sought other relationships with boys closer to my age, but none of those relationships could fill the deeply penetrating wound that festered in my soul.

With each relationship, I learned many lessons about what I did not want in my future husband. I was young and inexperienced when I opened the door to this lesson of courtship and was introduced to a power inside myself that I hadn't known before. I wanted to give of my love from within to another person and I was crushed when my first love just made a 180 degree turn and refused what was pure and precious from me. I felt the pain of heartache and a broken heart.

In a couple of other relationships, I learned just the opposite, of what it's like to have someone who was excessively possessive of me and wanted to have power and control over my life. I did not want to be married to anyone who prevented me from being who I am. I was happy with who I was, I just wanted someone who could enhance my life with the good qualities which I lacked.

Two
Unexplained Phenomena

"If you disbelieve me when I talk about the
things on earth,
how are you to believe if I should talk about
the things of Heaven?"
John 3:12

After I graduated from high school, my family moved to North Carolina and my life started anew. I attended community college and worked in the local bank as a teller. I continued to live with my parents and dated a few more men until I felt that with each relationship that followed was just more emotional roller coasters that were taking me nowhere. Then, I suddenly remembered the list of characteristics that I wanted to find in my future husband that I had contemplated about when I was around eleven to twelve years old. I had forgotten that I had thought this out with a list and I thought that perhaps the reason I was having bad luck in my courtships was because I had forgotten the logic part of my mind. Was I slipping into the same pattern other people did by following just my heart? I reasoned that I need to get back to my list to protect my heart from further damage and I became more secure in accepting my 'list.' I was not interested in dating a lot of men. I just wanted to find my future husband, and feeling intensely lonely and melancholy, I hoped that would be soon.

About four months later, a teller at the same bank where I worked asked me to visit her at her parents' home and her older brother was home from college, watching basketball on the living room TV. I felt at home with their friendly hospitality and noticed the strong family bond they shared.

A few weeks later, another coworker asked me to go to a party to meet people since I was new to North Carolina. When I drove myself to the party, she was nowhere to be found. But who I did find was the other teller's brother, Jack. He was very gracious and a gentleman. He helped me look for my friend but we found out that she had been there earlier, but then had left. But it worked out for me because as we talked I was immediately drawn to his comforting presence. Jack asked me out on a date and since I had previously met him at the other teller's home, I felt safe with him.

On our first date, we went out for dinner in a quaint, cozy restaurant. We got along very well and I was impressed with his polite courtesy. While we talked I was fascinated to find out that Jack loved history and could effortlessly tell me dates, facts and events about most anything around the world. This caught my attention because now I was trying to stick to my 'list.' I was utterly amazed with his memory of events in world affairs. Jack was like a walking encyclopedia about historical facts. Then, I saw that he had much confidence and wasn't shy to speak up in public. In fact, he loved to talk.

Next on my list was to find out how he

thought about his status in the world. What were his goals for the future? Jack told me that he was content with who he was and deliberately chose to remain middle class. He regularly attended church every Sunday and took some religious courses in college. Jack was tall, strong, sensitive, caring and such a gentleman. He had no interest in using drugs and seemed to be on the same path as what I was wanting to find according to my 'list.'

We dated for over a year and we got along beautifully. We never had any cross words or complaints with each other. I was hopeful that I had finally met the one I'm to marry and hoped that our relationship would heal my wounded heart. I thought that I was cautious to select someone who fit the good qualities which I lacked, but admired. At this time, both of us worked full-time. I now worked for the school system and he worked as a formulator and chemist.

When I turned twenty, we got married, moved into an apartment, and nearly two years later had our first child. Our apartment felt cramped so we moved out and bought our first house. It was a remodeled three-bedroom brick ranch style house in a rural community. Although we decided to buy this house, my intuition led me to believe we were making a mistake. There was something about that house that made me feel odd and uneasy. We lived there for more than six years, from 1983-1990, but I never had a restful sleep in that house. So many mysterious occurrences happened there that I eventually became accustomed and accepted the incidents with indifference. Although I didn't know or understand why they happened, these spiritual phenomena have opened my mind to things I would not have known otherwise.

Many nights I would stay up late at night while my husband and son slept without any difficulties. I would sit in a chair most of the time reading the Bible or watching late night television until I felt comfortable enough to sleep. All the lights were out in the house except for one living room lamp where I sat. On many occasions I felt the sensation of drifting up high above my chair toward the ceiling, but my body did not physically move at all. This is a mysterious sensation as though I had separated from my body. I enjoyed feeling this sensation and was astounded each time it occurred. I would look down toward my book and to the floor and it would seem I was floating ten feet above. Slowly, my sensation would descend back to the chair as I was truly sitting. It wasn't until decades later that I heard about astral travel, astral projection and out-of-body experiences. Was the experience I had the same thing?

* * *

I also began seeing and sensing numerous odd incidents. I cannot recall the order in which each occurred, but they were brief and happened repeatedly over the years that I eventually grew accustomed to them and accepted them. I was fed a teaspoon at a time of spiritual wonders, and tasted different forms of another realm of existence.

One evening while reading and everyone else was asleep, I heard someone walk up the hallway and stop beside me to the left side of my chair. I placed my finger on the end of the sentence I was reading, then looked over my left shoulder expecting to see my little boy of two years old. There was no one there! I called out my son's name, "Justin?" There was no answer so I got out of my chair to look down the hallway around the corner, still expecting to see my son. Again, I saw no one. Then I walked down the hallway toward his bedroom and called, "Justin... Justin?" I looked into his bedroom and found him sound asleep on his bed all covered up with his blanket. I was puzzled. Who walked up the hallway? I looked directly across the hallway into my bedroom and saw Jack sound asleep, snoring. I felt bewildered. Who or what were the footsteps I heard walk step by step up the hallway and stop next to me? I even felt a presence beside me. I quickly decided to get into bed with my husband, but I had to go back to the living room and turn off the light. I turned the hallway light on first. I ran to the living room and switched off that light. Then, I turned the hallway light off with the switch near my bedroom, jumped into bed, pulled up the blankets to my head, and squeezed right next to Jack. This brought back to mind an incident that I had as a young child. I felt the same way as when I saw a ghost between my brother's bedroom and mine, except now I'm a grown woman. Those sounds were beyond any simple creaking sound a house could make! I guess I'm learning more 'footsteps' about the spiritual realm.

Time passed by and I became somewhat accustomed to strange happenings. One day I was sitting on the living room floor wrapping a gift. I laid my scissors on the floor beside my right thigh to grab some ribbon. When I reached to pick up the scissors, they were gone. I searched the entire area, stood up, and moved all the wrapping paper, etc., but the scissors were nowhere to be found. I went to the kitchen drawer where I normally kept the scissors stored, then searched the kitchen counter and table. The scissors were gone. I returned back to my section in the living room to look again on the floor. Still, no scissors. I sat down, closed my eyes, and being annoyed, I spoke out loud, "I need my scissors! This is not funny. I'm not in the mood to play around. Give me back my scissors!" I placed my hand on the floor beside my right thigh, and the scissors were there! Now, you tell me how this happened! Disgusted and surprised at the same time, I said, "Thank you," and finished wrapping my gift. Creepy!

Three
My Life Turned Upside Down

"Happy the man who remains steadfast under trial, for having passed that test he will receive for his prize the gift of life promised to those who love God"
James 1:12

Since the birth of my son, I felt so happy to take on motherhood. I tried to be a good wife and a good mother, keeping up with the household chores of cooking and cleaning, tending to my beautiful baby boy, and all that a wife does. My husband wanted me to continue to work full-time because we needed the income to pay bills but my heart wouldn't let me give in. He wanted it his way which was completely opposite and against the grain of my heart. I wanted to stay at home as

18

much as possible with my child because I valued rearing children by their parents over child care, even with the sacrifice of doing without things. Material things do not compare to priceless moments of watching your own children grow and being involved in their daily development. I looked forward to being a mom and this was something that I placed at the top priority of my life. I wanted to be the best mother I knew how to be; to teach, nurture and bring him up with moral values. I thought a good compromise was for me to work part-time but Jack wasn't happy with that either so we continually fought over this issue.

My husband and I didn't see eye to eye and our relationship became very strained. My emotions deteriorated as our marriage took on many sad and discouraging problems from that point on. My hopes of raising my son in a peaceful, secure atmosphere suddenly flipped around. Jack began obsessing over any possibility of anyone in our family getting hurt or ill. He increasingly revealed signs of obsessive compulsive disorder, or 'OCD.'

Before we married, he told me that he had OCD, but he hadn't shown signs of anything too unusual in the three years of our relationship. I had never heard of it before, but from what I had observed, there seemed to be nothing to worry about. I was naive of any difficult situation developing.

OCD is a neurobiological disorder caused by the imbalance of the serotonin level in the brain which causes some paranoia and emotional outbursts. Jack had no control over his psychological compulsions and began cursing, having fits of rage, became over-bearing and controlling.

Jack began to change into someone quite different and showed me a part of himself which I hadn't seen before in our three-year relationship. He began interrogating me with the same questions every day upon coming home from work. Jack would ask: "Who did you talk to today? ... Did we have any phone calls? ... Did you go anywhere? ... Who did you see today? ... What did they say? ... What did you say? ... Why didn't you ask them such and such?" Then he'd start to put words in their mouth and I explained that they did not mention that. Then Jack would put words in my mouth and I explained that I did not say or do what he just said that I did. This interrogation became so irritating and overwhelming for me to carry on with such senseless discussions about things that didn't even happen! Having to deal with this day after day and month after month was emotionally draining for me.

Jack talked on and on until my mind was devoid of peace and I wasn't able to think what I wanted to think about and my memory began to suffer. I couldn't keep track of anything without writing it down. One day blended into any other day and I couldn't keep track of time. My mind even blanked out while I was driving on the roads I had traveled many times before.

Jack had an intense obsessed compulsion of thoughts that appear to be senseless; counted objects in his head, did rituals of turning things on and off over and over before he could leave the house. He told me all these things stem from OCD, but I never witnessed such mental torture before. He progressively became worse and threw things in the house and punched holes in the walls and doors. I didn't know how to handle this situation and my feelings toward him turned to fear and regret that I married him. I encouraged Jack to see a doctor, but he refused to take any medication. His behavior was affecting me by being at the end of his emotional 'whip.' My life was turned upside down and I felt that I was suddenly thrust into an insane situation. I did not want to live like this and I certainly did not want to raise our son in this environment.

As our relationship grew unbearable, many other problems with immediate family relations became difficult. His family which shone such a strong family bond only a few years ago had shattered. His parents eventually got divorced and their bitterness continued for years. Our siblings also had marital and financial problems. Dealing with my husband's paranoia, obsessive compulsive disorder, continual rants and stormy outbursts was very difficult and drained my energy. It was more than I could handle, and with the added stress of extended family issues was tipping me over the edge. I was becoming disgruntled and hopeless about my life and the world around me. I was overwhelmed and withdrew myself at home to sleep to avoid confrontation. I didn't feel like talking to anyone. It took effort to act happy, and I knew no one could help me anyway. I couldn't get enough peace or rest, and I descended into severe depression.

It seemed as though problems and traumas bombarded us repeatedly. I felt the drain of battle fatigue as if I were in the middle of a war zone. I was blasted from all sides. When would life start to turn around and be happy again? I know there are many people like us who go through some similar situations that we wonder why people just can't get along together. Why is it in human nature to be cruel to one another? In any event, these are some of the reasons why I escalated into a deep depression. My life wasn't what I wanted it to be and I felt victimized. I had tried to be so careful, but I had no better luck than anyone else. I begged God to let me know what to do. The harder I tried to find peace, it seemed the harder problems surrounded me. But why?

I could not rest with peace of mind for years. I slept very lightly and woke up from the slightest noises. As time passed by, I began to see partial glimpses of comforting apparitions. Upon immediately opening my eyes, I'd see a person or fragment of a person as they instantly dissipated into the darkness. I have no explanations of these. I wondered if my sudden waking from sleep could make me see things but the dream I had immediately before I awoke had absolutely no relevance to any apparition at the time I awoke. I could still remember the dream as it was still fresh in my mind, and it had nothing to do with this apparition.

Sometimes I would just wake up without any disturbance or noise and still, I would see an image for a split second. I wasn't actually looking for them when I suddenly awoke, and I never felt threatened or frightened by them, but how am I seeing them? I only grew curious as to why they appeared and considered that perhaps I only imagined them. I tried to analyze when I would see them but they would appear at no consistent intervals. Sometimes only a week or two would go by, or sometimes months between episodes. But, as time moved on, after repeated incidents, I realized that there is nothing I can do to stop anything spiritual from appearing. All I can do is accept them and I concluded that they must be real.

I can recall on one occasion of being comforted physically by one of these apparitions, or angels as I will call it because it showed loving feelings of reassurance and care. One night I went to bed extremely sad. I was sleeping on my stomach on the right side of my bed and facing my son's bedroom, straight across the hallway to the right. My son, being a toddler, commonly woke up during the night and came to our room to ask to come into our bed to sleep. Although we allowed him many times to join us, we tried to explain to him that only sometimes we would allow him in our bed if he wasn't feeling well, trying not to make it an every night habit.

During the quiet stillness of the night, I was awakened by a gentle, soothing hand patting my right hand. I thought my son was patting my hand to ask to join me in my bed. But when I opened my eyes, I saw a hand approximately the same size as mine right in front of my face patting my hand. It was not my husband's hand for he has very large hands. Besides, he was snoring behind me. The hand that I saw could have been either gender, but it was definitely an adult hand. I was not alarmed, but felt comforted by its reassuring gesture of concern for me. I sensed that this *being* wanted only to dissolve my worries. I could not see an arm or any other part of a body; only a right hand. Then it dissolved and blended into the night. I smiled, felt some peace, then drifted back to sleep.

I couldn't count how many times I awoke suddenly in the night to find or hear something move as if someone else was there watching over us. I would wonder about them each time it happened, but then I'd fall back to sleep because it was in the middle of the night and I was too sleepy to question what it was. I was becoming accustomed to these episodes. They were all peaceful and I did not fear any of them. Perhaps this was my Guardian Angel. I must thank God for sending my Guardian Angel for the many comforts of love!

***

I think that it is interesting to note that I had many episodes of déjà vu at this time in my life. It wasn't until an event happened that I recognized it as a memory of the future from a dream I had weeks or months earlier. One event is when my mother-in-law asked me to join her to listen to an orchestra in a neighboring city. It wasn't until I sat down in my chair, beside her in the audience that I had remembered seeing the exact same thing before. I had a dream weeks earlier where I saw myself watching an orchestra with my mother-in-law in the exact same chairs and the exact same room. How could I have foreseen this? Then the dream flashed to where I saw myself playing my saxophone in the orchestra. The dream ended seeing myself play on a stage during a concert.

In real life, after watching the concert, my mother-in-law and I joined the orchestra. We rode together every week for more than two years and played in malls at Christmas time, rest homes and festivals. I truly enjoyed playing in this orchestra for I hadn't played in a band since graduating from high school.

My mother-in-law and I eventually grew tired of driving out of town once or twice every week in the evening. We wished there were a closer orchestra in our hometown. My last concert was on a stage in a retirement center. As I sat down in my chair just as our concert began, the memory of my dream flashed in my mind as I remembered that my dream ended with this very concert.

Everything was just as the dream. I pushed the déjà vu back in my mind to contemplate later, because our concert was about to start. But I felt like jumping up in awe because I acknowledged to myself that I had miraculously foreseen this event!

Later, I pondered why déjà vu happens to so many people. Why and how can a person dream or remember something that hasn't taken place yet? There must be meaning into this phenomenon. How can people explain foreseeing the future?

Another time, I went into a department store which unexpectedly had a chocolate counter. I've never been in this store before, but, as I looked at the assortment of chocolates behind the glass case, my mind flashed a memory of this same exact moment. I recalled selecting particular chocolate tortes and had them boxed to give to my mother-in-law, my husband, and one for myself. I stood for a moment and said to the sales lady at the counter that this was a déjà vu moment and I wondered if I should follow my memory or change the event. She looked at me queerly, but I didn't care because I was telling her the truth. After pondering about it, I decided to follow the déjà vu and bought the same thing, just as I remembered. When I went home and gave out the candy, I told them this was a déjà vu incident, but I couldn't understand what the significance of buying chocolates was about. This awareness of déjà vu must be a lesson for some purpose, but what?

Four
Ultimate Joy!

"Many when they see will be filled with awe
and learn to trust in the Lord"

Psalms 40:3

This chapter is about my Near-Death-Like Experience which occurred in 1984, just 22 months after the birth of my son. At the time of this event, I had never heard about the Near-Death-Experience (NDE), or the Out-of-Body-Experience (OBE). Everything that I experienced was completely unexpected and it is a pure miracle of God. I've tried to describe every detail as best as I can, although no words can portray the full feeling of intense emotion that I felt. I only wish I could have you feel this with me. There is so much to tell and it is quite difficult to fully express the whole experience in its intensity. I will try my best, but I know that there are no words that will ever do it justice. I feel I must describe it in the present tense to transport readers into my experience to help them visualize step by step what I experienced as it unfolded. Read it slowly and place yourself in my place as I lead you into my story. This is exactly what I experienced which is the most exhilarating feeling of ecstasy any person could ever experience.

It is in the evening when my son, nearly two, is soundly asleep in his bed and my husband also retired early. The house is still and quiet and I feel all alone. I decide to take a shower before going to bed to try to revive myself from exhaustion, worry and tension. I let the warmth of the water hit my face and on top of my head for long moments, trying to wash away my sorrow. I close my eyes and take long deep breaths to exhale my sadness. I feel barely alive as I want to cry except there are no more tears from the well. I've struggled through the fight until I just can't do it anymore. I just can't seem to shake off my hopeless despair of sadness which never found comfort and lingered for years. I had squeezed out every last drop of emotional pain until I felt totally deplete of any energy and emotion. Tonight I have hit rock bottom. I have felt absolutely numb of emotion for nearly an entire year and I saw no way out. I felt no joy in my life. There were only constant problems. "I cannot take any more!" my soul screams but silent within me.

After drying off with effort and slipping on my night clothes, I directly check on my son who is still soundly asleep and then go to bed myself. I still feel all alone in my pain. I sullenly slip beneath the blanket and begin my prayer to our Lord with slow deliberate words. Each word takes each breath away even though I pray in silence. I plead with God for help and I tell Him exactly my dilemma. I have no enthusiasm, no will, nor strength to do anything. Everything that I do takes effort. I feel like a robot, so empty inside and I don't want to talk with anyone. I just want to hide and sleep. I am always tired and I do not want to get out of bed in the morning. I want simply to die. I pray the following:

*"Dear Lord, our Heavenly Father, I need your help. I am without any emotions. I cannot feel anything. If someone were to hit me or hurt me, I would not cry; I would not feel any pain. You know all I've gone through and I know you know how I feel now. My baby is so dear and yet, even he cannot make me smile. He giggles and does things I know I should feel happy about, yet I feel nothing. No happiness, nor sorrow. I have no more tears to cry . . . the well is dry. I have no enthusiasm; no will nor strength to do anything. I do not want to talk with anyone. I want to hide . . . I am tired . . . always tired. I do not want to get out of bed in the mornings. You know, Lord, I've been **this** down for over a year. I've tried and tried to get myself back emotionally. I can't do it! I don't know how. What else do I need to do? There is no one; not my husband . . . not my parents . . . no friend . . . no relative . . . preacher, or anyone who can help me. There is nothing anyone can say or do to help me. I*

*am alone. Lord, it is terrible! It is pitiful that my baby cannot make me feel a smile. I smile falsely to people so they think I'm fine. I smile when it is expected, but there is no feeling behind it. Lord, it is better for my son to have another mother than me who feels nothing. I am a robot. I move and think and eat . . . an empty box. I am worthless the way I am. No one can profit from me like this. Lord, it is in your hands. Do with me what you will. I am no good to anyone. I'm better off to be gone. I can't help myself. Lord, only **you** can help. There is no one else."*

Then as I give up my last weary hope to God, I conclude with the Lord's Prayer: *"Our Father, who art in Heaven, hallowed be thy name. Thy kingdom come, thy will be done on earth as it is in Heaven. Give us this day our daily bread and forgive us our trespasses as we forgive those who trespass against us. And, lead us not into temptation, but deliver us from evil. For thine is the kingdom, and the power, and the glory forever and ever! Amen."*

After I examine how I feel and explain to God that I didn't know how to get out of this slump of numbness, I hand my life over to Him. My heart feels tired and empty. I am heavy burdened and holding on by a thin thread about to snap. I give my all to God and my heart feels purely to the bottom of the essence of *need*. I give up my last weary hope to God as I fall asleep.

The next thing that I remember is waking up and finding myself on my knees and my head is facing down. "Where am I? I'm not in my bed," I wonder to myself. As I try to recognize my whereabouts, my head lifts up to see an oaken, wooden door that reminds me of the old school house door when my mom took me to first grade on the first day of school. The door was so huge with a presence of authority and respect. As I examine the door, trying to make sense of where I am, I notice there are no knobs. It had two doors that push open.

When my head is facing straight forward, I am now instantly standing but I don't remember using my legs to stand up. I look through the right-hand door with a window opening one foot high by two feet wide. As I look through the window, a torrential flow of excitement, joy and love bursts through me as I behold . . . our God! I know instantly who He is. I understand heart to heart as it is inherent and obvious that this Being is our Father. As my enthusiasm escalates, the doors, nearly six inches in thickness, invite me inward.

Instantly as the doors crack open, I hear music which nothing on Earth can compare. All of the Earth's symphonies pale in comparison. It sounds loud and piercing as a trumpet, yet the notes glide smooth as a violin, and also sweet pitched as a flute. It is all of these rich sounds blended perfectly as one. As I concentrate on the music, it gracefully slows down to a soothing lullaby. It could lull any colicky baby off to sleep. The effect is the most beautiful and emotionally soothing song I have ever heard.

As I focus on the mesmerizing beauty of the music, it flows through my body and I believe I hear it from within my whole self, not just my ears.

I don't know how to describe this sense of hearing. It is different from normal hearing. It feels like wind flowing through me and it seems to feel my emotion. I notice that the music began bursting forth with loudness and excitement as I had felt upon first seeing our Father, then the music became calm and tranquil as I listen and focus on the melody. Somehow this music became a dance between my thrilling emotion and a calming effect to bring me tranquility. It was so beautiful!

Next, I focus on how extremely bright my surrounding is, as though I am inside the sun surrounded by whiteness. Imagine being inside a light bulb, and yet the brightness doesn't hurt my eyes or cause them to squint. I can see every detail so clearly and sharp. The focus is precise and perfect. I had never seen anything with this much precision and clarity.

Then, I notice how healthy I feel. I am truly happy! There is **no** pain. My body feels light and free somehow. I sense a presence of others to the left and behind me. I feel their love and satisfaction of me radiating from their heart. I can actually feel *their* happiness and admiration emanating toward me without looking at them. Somehow I also sense their smiles even though I never take my eyes off of our Father to look at them. I assume that I will have a chance to look at the others later. I only want to see God right now! Nothing else matters to me. He sits before me on a throne. He is beautiful . . . magnificent . . . glorious! I've never seen any so breathtakingly wonderful! How can I possibly describe His Glory and this joy! There just are not any words to convey His Majesty! I was in speechless wonderment!

My heart is so full of excitement and love that my joy overflows as a flood. I am overcome by the intensity of love that I have never felt before. This feels so magical and exhilarating! I cannot hold back the flow of my emotion as I look upon Him with His face aglow with rosy cheeks, shining skin that reminds me of colored quartz crystal, with the glow of perfect health. I try to focus on the color of God's face but I have difficulty identifying it because it quickly fluctuated between all the hues of skin tones. It was like a dimmer switch that smoothly glides between fair to tan to ruddy tones with effervescent qualities. He isn't what I expected to see. I thought that He would be as perhaps an ancient looking Moses with a long shaggy white beard. He is very modern, strong and up-to-date with His majesty. His hair is pure snow-white and perfectly neat, as though He had just left the barber shop. He is perfect in every way! So beautiful! He is dressed in white as bright as light. I look at Him and understand without a doubt that He is everyone's Father, although He didn't *say* so. His Name is an all-embracing concept that I *knew* in my heart. I feel implicitly that He is our creator from whom ALL people originated.

As I stand in awe in His presence, God nods to me and without restraint, I enthusiastically lunge straight forward unencumbered, through the air as though I can fly. I do not sense my legs, although I am not concerned with myself as I glide straight ahead. I never look left or right. I instantly leap into His arms to embrace Him in pure love! The joy is beyond anything I had ever imagined or felt before!

The music shot up loud and vibrant as before with enthusiasm and I see myself with three views darting from one view to the other, then another; around and around like a spinning top! All three views dart from one to the other again and again so quickly that I am feeling dizzy. I see myself embracing Him upon His chest, all the while looking into His face only inches away, and I also view from a distance away behind myself watching our embrace in full view. What is this experience? The views just keep spinning faster than I can handle. This is unlike anything I had ever encountered. As I thought this, suddenly the merry-go-round of views stop. I feel as though I have just gotten off of an exciting roller coaster only this thrill was much more intense. I don't know how to describe the thrill.

I feel energy like electricity surging inside Him as we embrace. He embraces me in return with His arms. There is no way I can feel any happier than this very moment! I am swimming in divine love! We embrace for what seems to be thirty-seconds or so, (it's difficult to tell how long) and I never want to leave Him. Then I realize that all the hardship in my life was worth this moment. I cannot describe how intense my emotion feels. It is indescribably wonderful! This is ecstasy!

Since I was about ten years old, I couldn't wait until I could finally meet God face to face and just hug Him! I've always had the need to hug Him but I thought that that time would be after I die. And now, finally, I had my wish come true. It is possible! Ever since I was young I wanted to have a relationship with God and an opportunity to see or hear him, and I succeeded! Now I want to find the blueprints that lead me to God so that I could help others find Him as well. All we had to do was to look for Him with all our heart, mind and soul, and He was there! I am still astonished that He permitted me, a speck of a person, to hug Him. Wow! Who am I that He would allow to touch

Him? How can this be? I *know* how much He loves each and every one of us no matter how minute or prominent we may be in our life on Earth. This is beyond my comprehension that He would do such an extraordinary wonder for me.

The scriptures were right! Acts 17:27 states; *"They were to seek God, and, it might be, touch and find Him."* And John 14:17 & 21 states; *"The world cannot receive him, because the world neither sees nor knows him; but you know him, because he dwells with you and is in you . . . and he who loves me will be loved by my Father; and I will love him and disclose myself to him."* This is surely possible.

But then, I begin to question without speaking, "I must have died (because I am truly in Heaven). But, how did I die? Oh, no! It must have been instantly . . . like a bomb! Oh, no! The people! The Earth! A bomb must have killed us all. Is everyone gone?" My heart sinks down with empathy for what I thought had passed away. I begin to feel tribulation about the people. God knew how I felt and He gently stretched out His arm, while still holding me with the other (like a loving Father), and spoke to me the only words I heard Him speak, "Everything is all right." His voice is perfect and calming and I know immediately that the people were safe with God as He reassures me that it is okay. I stop worrying, but I still think that the world that I knew is now gone.

I sense that it is time for me to go with a man who sat to the side of God whom I hadn't noticed before. I am not alarmed that he is suddenly there. It is not revealed to me why he is there but his visual looks are of someone that I knew on Earth. I think it odd that he only *looks* like the person but did not *feel* to be the person he looked like. I wonder if perhaps he is in a disguise. I truly know that God has the power to do *anything* and *everything*. This must have some deep lesson for me, but right now, I'm not sure what the intended lesson is. I suppose this person was shown to me for my purpose alone, between me and God.

This man who suddenly appeared beside

God seems as though he had watched us throughout my entire visit, but with no expression on his face. I cannot sense any feelings from him yet I recall feeling love radiating from others around us which I still did not get to view since I would not consider looking around or behind myself. This man stands up and holds out his right hand to me. I know that I am supposed to go with him and I assume that he will take me to where I belong in Heaven.

Slipping away from God, I slowly arise and begin to take hold of this man's hand. Instantly, even before I touch his hand, I feel myself return back into my body on Earth. If I had known this, I would not have reached for his hand! Why didn't God warn me that I was leaving Him! I suppose I was meant to return because if I had known that I would return to Earth, I would have refused to go. But why was I sent back? There must be a reason that I had to return.

My body is lying down on my bed, face-up. I instantaneously slip through my chest and I feel my soul disperse throughout my entire body. I flow like liquid into my arms, all the way down to my fingertips, and into my legs, all the way to my toes. For about thirty-seconds I lie in bed and can feel my skin surround me as though I am being enclosed in a body glove or a molded cage. My body is my container, a coating surrounding my spirit. I can feel both of them separately as I tingle with warmth. Then my body and soul blend together as one, like a sponge absorbing water. My body becomes one with my soul. I lie there **wide awake**, alert, and full of excitement! My heart is still pounding with ecstasy!

As I lie in bed, I am astonished! "I saw God! OUR FATHER!" My heart is pounding with a speed so fast that it feels it could burst, physically, from the extreme excitement! I look to the left and I see my husband asleep. I wonder what time it is as I try to acknowledge my homecoming or 'earth-coming.' I get up from my bed to look at the clock on my dresser and it is now that I realize that my eyesight has returned to how it was so that I cannot see without eyeglasses or my contact lens. The lighted digits on the clock shows 4:00 a.m.

***

Many people argue that God cannot be seen or even look human. I don't have an explanation. All I can say and testify is how I witnessed God in my experience. Perhaps God chooses the way He manifests Himself to each individual person for whatever the reason. The Father Being which I saw may be different from what you will see one day, or maybe He will look the same. That doesn't matter to me as I believe that God may manifest Himself as He chooses to do.

I contemplated about the scriptures in the Bible. God had disguised Himself as a burning bush to Moses, and as a dove which descended upon Jesus as he was baptized by John the Baptist. I suppose that since all of creation was created in Him, then He can choose to manifest as whomever or whatever He wishes. Nothing is beyond God. God is truly boundless.

When God revealed Himself to Moses on

Earth, Moses had to hide in a crevice and he could only see the back as God passed by him. And the Old Testament states that Abram, Jacob and Hagar saw God. (Genesis 17:1-2, Genesis 28:13 & 32:30, Genesis 16:14) So, it must be possible to *see* God if only our frail bodies could handle it. I believe that God must choose to reveal Himself to us, but doesn't necessarily show everyone. That's not our choice or our control.

I don't want to argue with the testimony of another person about what they believe about God, but I cannot deny my experience. I am also aware of the controversies where the word God is used to put fear, shame and guilt in people. That is not my intent. It bothers me that some people may misunderstand why I use the word God. I don't think of 'God' as a name, but only as an inadequate word used to distinguish our Creator, our Source, the Beginning. This most loving Being who revealed Himself to me as 'our Father' did not introduce Himself to me. I did not ask who He is and He did not explain. I just knew in my heart that this is my spiritual Father as well as the spiritual Father of all people. I did not feel that religion had anything to do with it. I ask that those who read my books to know that I do not believe that God created any group of people to condemn others. Such prejudice is our own undoing.

This experience is intensely real – more so than my life on Earth. I can accept that we may not see God on the Earth realm, but this is Heaven! Surely it is expected to find God in Heaven! I seriously believe that if we saw God on Earth while we are in our mortal bodies, we might just explode upon seeing Him. Divine Love is that intense!

Another thing, Jesus was not recognized by his very own disciples after he was crucified.[1] And again when Jesus walked along the road with two men and Jesus asked them what had just taken place. The men wondered why Jesus (in disguise) hadn't heard of the crucifixion of the Lord.[2] Surely these men must have known what Jesus looked like, for they were there and saw him on the cross. Yet

---

1. John 21:1-14
2. Luke 24:13-24

49

Jesus was walking right beside them when they did not know who he was. Jesus wasn't recognized until after he broke the bread.[3]

"I know that thou canst do all things and that no purpose is beyond thee. But I have spoken of great things which I have not understood, things too wonderful for me to know."[4] Surely if Jesus disguised himself to the people, then also God can and may do the same. *"Many when they see will be filled with awe and will learn to trust in the Lord."*[5]

***

I lay back down in bed in awe and amazement to relish what had just happened to me. I was so anxious that I couldn't contain myself. "God let me be with Him! I can't hold it in! I must tell everyone in the whole world how wonderful our God is!" I felt like screaming from the tops of the

---

3. Luke 24:28-32

4. Job 42:2

5. Psalms 40:3

mountains! I had seen *"things beyond our seeing, things beyond our hearing, things beyond our imaging!"*[6] Oh how these scriptures are coming alive to me. I understand what they were talking about! The scriptures contain the truth and yet people do not clearly comprehend their depth.

I reached over to awaken my husband. "Jack! Jack! You won't believe what has happened! I was with God! Just now! I just felt myself return to my body." I told him all that you have just read. He listened so quietly that I thought he had drifted off back to sleep. "Jack! Are you awake? Did you hear me!" I questioned him with excitement.

"Yea," he responded politely, "I heard everything you said." I can't believe he stayed awake that long. Then he affirmed that he believed me. From that moment on, it's all I could think and talk about! Nothing else mattered to me. Nothing else was as important as this!

How can I possibly describe every detail to

---

6. 1 Corinthians 2:9 & 10

its full effect? I had seen, felt, and heard not as people do on Earth. I had a different sensory perception in Heaven that was richer and more in-depth with a heightened reality. It was a true essence of feeling free! How can I fully describe to others what people have not yet felt, heard, nor seen in the same way as I had? There is nothing in comparison on the Earth. I knew with an overwhelming conviction that my presence in Heaven was truer, past all comparison than my life on Earth. I now know that I was in the spirit and that my body entraps me to the Earth. It is my vessel and I am bound in captivity to the world. So this is what is meant by 'to set the captives free!' "Aha!"

This was in no way a dream! How can a dream sense what our life on Earth has not ever done before? How can a mere dream touch me so profoundly that it overtakes and changes my life! God had intervened in my life and cured me of my depression. He lifted it away and replaced it with love and a renewed life. It is a love so rich that I had not known it before in our realm. I am alive and replenished with emotion once again! I feel happy, and I can cry if need be. I am fine . . . I am okay. I am ME again only with a renewed energy and sense of purpose. Everything is all right!

I must thank God, our Father. I know that without His assistance I would never have beaten my depression. I would have only rotted away in spirit. It's been more than thirty years since this experience, and I must tell you that I have never come close to being as depressed as I was before this event. I have been sad, hurt, glad, thankful, etc., but never hopelessly stuck in depression. I can bounce back! I know without a doubt that there is more to our life than this domain on Earth. Thank you Father! How awesome you are!

As I lay there in bed after sharing this experience with my husband, I thought of how Mother Mary must have felt when she talked with an archangel and found that God had done a mighty and wondrous thing to her. Although my experience can never compare to hers, I felt this same joy and awe. I also found and experienced an amazingly loving God! Then, I thought of the many people who didn't believe her and couldn't comprehend how God works His miracles in the most humble ways. It is difficult for me to fathom that God would take a person such as me, before I have even died, and do such a miracle as allowing me to visit with Him in Heaven. How is this possible!!! It just boggles my mind! I must share my experience and hope that my testimony will help others and encourage them to believe in the existence of God. My experience also gives validity of many religious scriptures. Our God is an awesome God!

***

Now I truly know:

1. *"If you invoke me and pray to me, I will listen to you: when you seek me, you shall find me; if you search with all your heart, I will let you find me, says the Lord."*
(Jeremiah 29:12-14)

2. *"Those who love me I love, those who search for me find me."* (Proverbs 8:17)

3. *"He who finds me finds life."* (Proverbs 8:35)

Five
A Blessing and Overcoming Fear

"There is no room for fear in love;
perfect love banishes fear"
1 John 4:18

Two and a half years after my encounter with God, I had my second child. She was so precious and delicate, and I was so happy to have a daughter. I had a very fast delivery of only two hours of labor. The doctor told me that I must hurry and push hard to force her out because the umbilical cord was wrapped around her neck and she was in duress, otherwise he would have to do an emergency caesarean. I pushed with all I had and she was delivered with my last breath and last strenuous push.

She was born healthy and everything

seemed fine until late that evening. I awoke in the middle of the night and just had to check on my baby during her first night. I walked over to view the babies and I saw a baby in an incubator. This baby had tubes attached to her mouth and enclosed in a see-through casing. My baby was fine earlier that morning with no indication of any trouble when she was born. The nurse looked startled at me and said, "She'll be all right." It was then that I realized it was my baby! Why didn't anyone tell me? She had breathing difficulties, probably from the cord that was around her. The nurse insisted that I take a sleeping pill so I could rest and recuperate from the labor. Even then, I could not sleep that night. I worried and waited for the pediatrician to check her again very early the next morning in search of the source of her problem. He decided to transfer her to another hospital that specialized in baby and child care. My husband and I went with her to the other hospital in another city. We traveled back and forth every day and stayed as long as we were permitted. Why was my baby born with problems? I lived day by day in numbness. Finally after a week, she was released. We were finally able to take our baby home!

Then when she was five weeks old, she had Pyloric Stenosis, which we were told was rare for a baby girl and being only five weeks old. She could not hold down anything she drank and threw it up with projectile force, thoroughly drenching my clothes; so again she was admitted to the same specialized hospital. This time, I was able to sleep in a chair in her room. I stayed with her day and night, never leaving her. Again, I was in shock and refused to cry. My husband and I were so exhausted and numb when we finally were able to bring her home once again and resume our normal life. We were afraid to relinquish our anxiety for fear of another tragedy.

Through all our worrying, I am amazed that I never returned to the depressive state I felt before my Near-Death-Like Experience. I felt so grateful that the Lord gave me strength to endure and so I continued to focus on the church and placed working for the Lord in my foremost priorities. I delve into teaching Sunday Church School and other children's church activities. My children were with me most of the time at the church whenever they could. My husband supported my works at church by watching our children whenever I couldn't. He saw the importance of my work and knew that I loved what I did. My work for the Lord was my plumb line to happiness. The Lord's presence was with me in my works as everything I did in Christ's work prospered and gave me joy as I knew I was following the right path. The effect of my efforts was alive in the children of the church as they became more involved with church activities. Their interest in church grew along with their attendance.

But as my life was given joy as I fulfilled a purpose for the Lord, my personal family life still pulled against the core of my being and drained my joy. I still felt that I was in a constant battle to recover from the emotional blows. Jack continued to have so many harsh outbursts and tantrums related to his obsessive compulsive disorder that repeatedly pushed me to my limit again. My heart was emotionally torn asunder. I couldn't live with the wall of choice I was repeatedly forced to decide about my marriage. Since this problem would not go away, I had to make a decision to either stay married or divorce. Divorce was a choice that I just couldn't make because I did not want a broken family. How could I be assured that that was the correct choice? I wish I could see into the future, but I had to make my decision by chance.

I finally sought counseling in hopes of finding the best solution, so I asked our church minister to visit during the day to discuss my problem. I shared with him all of the emotional draining that I endlessly endured. I was in duress and felt trapped in a nightmare. I lived each day living in fear of my husband's anger and worrying for my son. Just as soon as Jack left for work, I could feel a black cloud leaving with him. That black, ferocious cloud returned each time Jack returned home. We never knew when lightning would strike or how violent the storm would be. Although Jack has never physically harmed me, I was emotionally traumatized.

After an hour long discussion, my minister told me that I did deserve better and that the Lord gives us the choice to change our lives, and He forgives our sins. After the minister left, I contemplated on what he said. I thought to myself, Jesus deserved better, but look what he chose to do. He was beaten and crucified for committing no sin. He persevered to the end.

I am not perfect and have sinned in my life, so I should expect some problems. Nobody wants to live a life filled with pain and suffering, but Jesus accepted what the world gave him. Why should I think that I should have it any easier on Earth? We are to carry our own crosses and try our best to follow in his footsteps. I felt that most people would have probably chosen divorce, but somehow I also felt that I need to keep fighting to overcome my problems. God may have revived my spirit to help me survive, but I still had to face the problems which had led me into depression and I didn't want to get stuck there again. Maybe I'm making a terrible mistake, but the alternative isn't much better from what I can see.

***

The day arrived when my son was entering first grade on August 23, 1989. I was excited for my son and wanted this day to be happy for him. Instead, the day started off on the wrong foot. I was awakened by my moody and argumentative husband complaining yet again. I never knew when or why he would be triggered to blow up, but it always managed to be at the most inopportune times. I suppose he was nervous about our son going to school for his first day, and he couldn't get a grip on his obsessive-compulsive behavior. Another 'would be' special moment in the life of my son was shot to smithereens! Why does Jack ruin the joys in our life?

It takes me a good hour to wake up in the morning before I feel alert and ready enough to carry on a conversation, or argument, in this case. Quiet mornings were scarce, for this was the time of day when my husband commonly raged in his booming, gruff voice. My heart stung with each word he spoke and I could feel the energy drain out of me before I had a chance to awaken for the day. We had a very upsetting morning which caused me to feel sad all day. I cried most of the day as I felt very doubtful about where our lives were heading.

I stayed at home with our daughter because it really wasn't worth working part-time with two children. Day care and after-school care were so costly along with buying gas and car expenses, work clothes, etc. It didn't seem to pay off with all the hassle and I would have only broken even anyway. Besides, I still couldn't stand the thought of someone else raising *my* child. I wanted to raise her, to watch her grow, and teach her my ways. In my mind, I could not allow myself to give up my role of motherhood which I longed for more than anything else I could do in my life. I compromised and worked half-time with my first child. This time

I won't permit Jack to take away my opportunity to be the mother I want to be. This was my life too! I knew that if I went back to work full-time, that I would regret it for the rest of my life. If he forced me into this, I would have no honor for not standing up for myself and for my children. To go back to work at this time in my life would totally demolish any remaining hope I had left in our marriage and also in my life. This was my absolute last straw to hang onto my marriage with Jack. For me, to give up motherhood for a work career would be a death sentence and I refused to sever my last string of hope for survival. It was either I stay home and raise our children or we were getting a divorce! He did not want a divorce, so the decision was that I stayed home.

That evening I couldn't sleep because I was still carrying the pain of our quarreling in my heart. This argument began with the birth of my first child and it never ended even though I gave Jack an ultimatum of a divorce. I was too sad and needed to consult with Jesus about my disappointments again.

I looked outside and all was still and quiet. It was a very hot August evening and we didn't have air conditioning in our home. I turned the floor fan on and faced it to blow onto me. As I sat on the sofa in front of the open living room window, I talked to Jesus for over a half hour with only the moon shining on me for light. I begged for Jesus to help me decide what I should do. I tried to visualize how Jack could be without Obsessive Compulsive Disorder. I realize that he is a good person, but he is tormented by this mental disorder that he couldn't escape. I could have lived easier with him if he didn't have OCD; I'm sure he'd be much happier without it also. I finally concluded to blame his tantrums, not on Jack, but upon the effects of being tormented by his condition and as someone who needed my help. Can I find the strength and endurance to meet this challenge?

It would take time and much more encouragement than I could muster until Jack would take the initiative and courage to open his eyes to see how he negatively affected us. It was difficult for him to realize that his behavior was traumatizing us. Every time I initiated a conversation in an attempt to resolve his anger, we always ended up bitter. It was hard for him to see himself through our eyes. Step by step, he eventually began to see where his mistakes and tantrums radiated out and affected others. Jack did not want to be as he was, but it was difficult for him to really try to improve, especially when he repeatedly denied his aggressive behavior. I worked hard just to get him to acknowledge his actions. He's moving at the pace he chose, and perhaps he will eventually move toward making less aggressive choices.

It was slow going but I had to learn patience which taught me endurance, which was another painful lesson. I gave Jack credit for his efforts when he did admit to want to do better and decided to endure this as 'my cross' to learn the virtue of endurance. I'm going to see this through to become my full potential of the qualities God wants to find in me. It is my hope that Jack will also become closer to his potential. Some trials take us as far as we choose to go until we find our breaking point, of which I've hit many times. Those are the times to grab tight to God and think about the examples He showed us through scripture to follow.

By always thinking about how Jesus endured his cross without deserving any of the traumatic horrors he went through, I didn't want to do the wrong thing in my life. I didn't want to be too weak to endure my hardship. I didn't want to disappoint God or His plan for me and our family's spiritual growth. I've got to trust God to work out our lives the way He wants it done, and not how I wanted it to be.

As I continued to intently pray to Jesus, drawing deeply from my heart, my husband and children were sound asleep. I was surrounded by stillness and silence until, all of a sudden, the fan on the floor which was only a couple feet away from me, revved up and vibrated as though something were restraining the fan from free flowing air. The fan gasped for air and became louder with suction noise. I turned my head away from the moonlit sky to look down at the fan on the floor. Someone was standing directly in front of it, within a foot away from me! I began to slowly scan upward, searching its long black cowl. Studying meticulously as I raised my eyes up toward the arms with its long sleeves concealing any hands, I searched further up to its head which was ensconced by an unrevealing hood. I saw only darkness in its face. Its robe fluttered from the fan. I could only stare as I was traumatized as a stone and couldn't move or yell. This presence never made a sound or movement beyond its wavering robe. I could feel my heart pound as I only heard the fan choking for air. It doesn't make much sense to me that the fan was choking while at the same time, blew enough wind to flutter its robe, but this is how it occurred. Just as I felt I could not stand another second of this ghastly sight, the visitor dispersed into the darkness and was no more to be seen. The fan instantly relaxed. I was terrified! I swear that if this creature had stayed another second, I would have had a heart attack from fear. I hurried and turned the fan off, then ran back to bed.

I kept wondering why this apparition came to visit me and how did it manifest from the spirit to the physical realm? The next morning, as I told Jack about it, he said; "It could have been the *mourner*."

I questioned him; "What does the mourner come for and why would it come to me? Was it mourning with me, or was it going to take me away?"

We couldn't resolve why it came. Maybe it came to warn me that our neighbor was soon to die only five days later, or was it the beginning of a disastrous dilemma, soon to be engaged? I do not know why it came, but I will always wonder. I won't ever forget the terror I felt for whatever its reason. I only hope it never returns for I do not want to feel the severity of the fear I felt again. I will always want answers, but I know I cannot ever know *why* for certain. I must go on with my life and try to place the fear behind me, or should I say; I must learn how to overcome the fear, however long this takes me.

Now I am forced to battle my trial of fear. Deep down in my heart, I still had a fear of the apparition I saw when I was a young child less than five years of age. Why did it appear? My fear and worry of choosing the wrong decisions in my life broke down my body to where I suffered asthma, and now the ultimate fear was manifested in my presence by this 'mourner'.

In recent years I've spoken to a couple of people who had also seen fiercely frightening creatures. One woman told me that she was writing a book and decided to give all of the profits to charity. After her decision, a huge ugly creature came out from her bedroom wall and loomed over her above her bed that night. It came directly up to her face and growled. She knew it came because it didn't like that she wanted to do good by giving all profits away to charity. She felt it was angered by her generosity of benevolence.

Another woman told me of a similar experience she had. She does not know the other woman who lives in my hometown. One night, after extensive and heartfelt prayers, she decided to give herself to God for whatever His purpose was without reservation. As she became quiet to go to sleep, an enormous deformed dog towered next to her in bed. (This reminded me of the other woman's story.) She felt the moist heat of its breath against her face as it snarled next to her ear with its drooling saliva. She was terrified and yet felt with conviction that its presence was actually an indication that she was doing something that it did not like. She was determined to do something significant for God. If she had enough good intentions that caused enough grief for this creature to find it worth its trouble to manifest, then she considered it a complement and an indication that she's on the right track.

I knew exactly their fear, although I had only seen a human form covered by a black cowl, like a monk. At the time it appeared, I was thinking about how Jesus decided to take his cross without deserving any of the traumatic horrors he went through, and also decided that I would take up my cross, no matter the suffering. Maybe this is why my fearsome manifestation came to knock me off my feet with fear. Perhaps it didn't like that I chose to suffer through the dilemma instead of giving up.

This event happened after being married for eight years, and now I've been married for more than thirty years. I've gone through very trying emotional trials, but through them, I've learned the virtues of patience, endurance, and a stronger bond to God. I know I can survive anything because He is with me. If the only way people can learn good virtues are through the hard work of conquering hard trials, then I've done my share! I have most definitely improved my virtues and I can be pleased without shame as I stand before the Lord as He reviews my life. I'll go through anything this world wants to dish out to me, because I know I'm going home one day with the joy of the triumphs of my lessons.

***

I've experienced innumerable doors of lessons and learned the wisdom to understand and know what I didn't know before. I am thankful for my trials because I see the results of my spiritual growth. I didn't like going through the fire as I still must endure, but I've learned to see beyond - to the gold refined by the fire. The point is, that even though I've made mistakes in my life, I've learned from them. The errors are not so humiliating as if I had not learned from any of them. It's almost impossible not to grow a little from our experiences on Earth, so everyone should look forward to what we become. This is why God forgives us. He knows growth comes through our mistakes and pain. He loves us and gives us so many chances to learn so we all have the opportunity to come to Him in His perfect glory.

Since perfect love banishes fear, I was shown that I had a battle to overcome. I wanted to develop perfect love as best as I could obtain and so was shown an area where I needed to focus my attention. I will take this aberration as a cue from

God and not wall up a barrier and cry defeat. I know that I need to work on overcoming fear.

I used to have a recurring dream about a ghost chasing me when I was a child. Being weary of running, I'd slow down as I reached an embankment. As I turned to face the ghost, it came within reach. I'd always wake up frightened at this point. This dream repeated so many times that I became bored with it. Knowing the dream so well, I began thinking about what would happen before it happened. I became separate from the participant in the dream and became an observer. Being aware that I was looking upon the dream as a spectator, this time I decided to change the ending. I became annoyed with the dream and angered by the ghost until I mustered the courage to stand up to the ghost without fear. This was the first time I'd completely conquered my fear and the dream never returned. Though there were no words needed in this dream, the control of our emotions was the lesson. I believe this dream was trying to tell me to face my fears head on and not be afraid.

It's also like the ghost was a representative of the devil. I was afraid to stand up to him and face the regrettable power which was only a myth. The devil had no control over me. It was all intimidation without strength. If he had any power, it was only because I gave it to him. After repeating the scene of terror (caused by my own insecurity), I finally became tired with the mundane repetition of episodes and developed the virtue of bravery and had the energy of confidence and courage. There are many things in the world that people avoid just because of their own fears. The end result isn't nearly as tragic as if I had not taken the courage to be brave. This dream tried to teach me to face my fears and try to have confidence and courage. With God leading me, everything will turn out fine in the end.

Six
I'm Not Alone

"No one knows the Father but the Son
and those to whom the Son may
choose to reveal him."
Matthew 11:27

Being a grown woman in my early thirties and mother of two children, I liked books, but could never bring my attention toward sitting down to read for very long, though I wished I could. I enjoyed being involved with activities that filled up my time, and I found it difficult to remain inactive for a period of time. One weekend while shopping at a mall with my husband, we happened to go into a bookstore. My eyes fell upon a blue book of a woman with her arms reaching into a bright light. It was on the bestseller's list and I was drawn to it because the woman resembled me exactly! This is how I looked when I was in Heaven with our Father God. I couldn't believe my eyes! Staring at the book in amazement at the connection of myself and this book, I read the description of what it was about and instantly recalled my own experience. I had to hold back my tears.

"I'm going to own this book, but I don't have enough money to purchase it right now. I'll come back and get it later," I thought to myself. The book was only in hardback, so since money is tight, I may have to wait until it comes out in paperback. I showed the book to my husband, hoping that he would purchase the book for me. He just nodded nonchalantly that I wanted it, but then said it was time to go home. He seemed to be uncomfortable about the book, which also made me feel that he was uncomfortable about my experience as well.

At this time in my life, I had gone back to work. The following day at work, during lunch break, one of my co-workers, Denise, blurted out,

"Have you read the book, <u>Embraced by the Light</u>?"
I stopped eating, shocked that she had just asked me about the book I was drawn to only yesterday in the mall. I answered her, "I just saw that book yesterday in a bookstore and I want to read it. What is it about?"

Denise said, "It's very good, and it makes me think. It's a story about a woman who has died and gone to Heaven. She returned to Earth after her near-death experience and told about what happened to her. Do you think something like that is possible?"

I gulped and answered, "Yes, (I paused to reflect whether I should explain further). I do believe that can happen. As a matter of fact, I kind of went through the same thing years ago. I have also gone to Heaven, except I did not die to my knowledge. My soul was separated from my body during the night. My soul went to Heaven, then returned back into my body through my chest. I was gone only minutes. I <u>know</u> it can happen."

We began discussing the subject and what

had happened to me in my experience. I felt joy inside myself to finally find someone else in this world who has gone through such an amazing experience such as mine, except I did not stay in Heaven nearly as long as Betty Eadie, author of Embraced by the Light.

Denise nodded and asked me, "Would you like to borrow my book to read about it?"

I joyfully responded, "Wow, that's great! You own the book! I'd love to read it. Thank you so much!"

Isn't it amazing that I didn't have the money to purchase the book the day before, and then the following day Denise offered to let me read her book! The synchronicity of this makes me think that I'm supposed to read it.

I showed her part of my journal where I finally wrote down my experience. I had waited nearly ten years after my experience happened before I could finally compose myself enough to write about it down on paper. Any time I'd recall the incident through the prior years, my thoughts carried me away into my memory. I wanted to relive it all over again and again in my mind and feel the total joy all over again. I yearned to repeat that experience because it was so wonderful. It took a long time until I could slow my mind down enough to write because my emotions from that experience still felt so intense.

I let Denise read my journal and she was very receptive and didn't think that I made it up. She said that I had written it very well with much detail. I was happy to find someone who believed me without acting distant toward me afterward. I was so excited that someone actually came to me and asked me about such an experience. I finally had an opportunity to openly share my experience and it felt good!

Of course, my family members whom I've told my story did not reject me, but I do not feel that they truly embrace my experience. They try to find an explanation that explains it to *their* liking. It's difficult to share with people, even when we know them well, when their hearts aren't open to it. It was so difficult for me to have such a strong desire to share my experience with others when I also learned that many people would reject it. Nobody understands what it feels like to be bursting with joy but then having to keep it all bottled up inside. The joy was like the bubbles in a carbonated drink bottle that is all shook up. It's hard to keep the bubbles from spewing forth.

My husband says that he believes me and knows that I am being honest. He lived with me when most of my spiritual experiences occurred and he saw how they affected me; he just doesn't understand them. How could he totally understand if he hadn't personally experienced it? My mom thought I had a very strong dream of some sort, and some friends have become estranged. I understand that all people are not ready to hear extraordinary spiritual truths. I have to not let those who don't believe bring me down. The only witness that truly matters to me is God and I will not deny Him.

I couldn't wait to read <u>Embraced by the Light</u>! As I read that evening after work, I found some similarities between Betty's experience and my own. I could really relate to her story and I was so happy not to be alone. I decided that I needed to write to Betty Eadie. I am more of a private person, and don't usually write to people, but I needed a connection with someone who understands this phenomenon.

At this time of my life, it was February of 1994. My experience happened in November of 1984. It sure didn't seem like nearly ten years had passed. It seems like only yesterday that I had been there, in Heaven. My memory was still so very strong and vivid as though it just happened. I felt more alive in the few minutes I'd spent in Heaven than in any time I had lived here on Earth. This is hard to explain to people because there is nothing to compare this with. It felt like a heightened sense of reality. I now do not fear dying because I know that after we leave our life on Earth, that's when we begin to really live in a much better place!

Though I had written to Betty Eadie, a response that I waited and hoped for, never came.

She only sent me her newsletter, *Onjinjinkta*. I was happy to receive her newsletter, and I knew she must be an extremely busy woman, but I needed to find someone who understood me and my experience. I needed to talk about it and to share with someone who also had a similar experience and would embrace what I needed to share from my heart without rejecting it. I don't know why this was so important for me, but I just couldn't let it go! Something was driving me from the inside.

A year later, I decided to write Betty another long heartfelt letter, but still no personal reply. I tried to put out of my mind the need to communicate with her and I focused on my daily life. I still had an urgency to find someone to fill a need in my life. Something's not quite right. I couldn't place my finger on what I needed to do.

My appetite for searching and reading books about religion, near-death and related experiences now began to catapult into an unending hunger to search for anything that would acknowledge my awareness and knowledge of God. I wanted to learn how other people were affected by visions, spiritual experiences, etc. I wanted to find and relate with others with similar experiences. Each book that I read led me to other books and more inquisitive questions. My mind was being drawn further and deeper in thought as I contemplated thoughts I'd never had before.

I began volunteering with Hospice patients and I went through training workshops and immunizations, hoping this would fill my longing of helping people. I was honored to be able to help adults and children during their personal health crisis. People have asked me how I could work with people who were ill and dying. They think it would be so depressing. I told them that the people I help are thankful for any assistance offered. They are kind and selfless. I wanted them to remember and experience kind gestures from a person who helped to ease their discomfort on this Earth, so they could have some dignity. I felt honored to be invited into their lives at such a personal time in their life. I knew that they were about to experience the awesome love of God in the light as I had done. They were closer to seeing God face to face than I was at that moment and I felt comforted by that. I knew where they were headed and inside I felt happy for them to be going home. They had suffered as warriors and learned many things from their lives and will receive rewards from God soon. They are finally going home to rest in peace and joy in the Heavenly realm, and hopefully, they've won a new, higher destiny.

Several weeks before one male patient passed away, he kept hearing music. He asked me where it was coming from. I couldn't hear any noise, but searched the entire house for radios, TV's, or anything else that might be left on. I looked outside, but could not find any music. I asked him what kind of music he heard. He said that it was country music. I thought this was a sign that he would be leaving Earth soon, but I didn't tell him. The following week, he became sicker and went to the hospital. After a couple weeks, he began to improve and the hospital considered releasing him. I went to visit him in the hospital, but he was asleep and I didn't want to wake him. I talked to him quietly for a while, but I knew he would pass away soon. Within a week, he was gone. I have learned that many people nearing death hear or see things that we don't before they leave. It seems to be a peaceful sign from God. It seems common for an ill person to improve just before they pass on. I saw this happen a number of times and I prepared myself because I knew they were going home to God. I was happy to be a part of their farewell journey.

Through volunteering with Hospice, I came across the book, The Case for Heaven[7], by Mally Cox-Chapman. It was about messages of hope as the author examined more than fifty people who touched eternity. It was such a great inspiration for me and it provided a source of additional spiritual research.

One day I purchased the Matthew Visual

---

7. Cox-Chapman, Mally. The Case for Heaven, Messages of Hope from People who Touched Eternity. New York: The Berkley Publishing Group, 1995.

Bible[8]. I immediately loved the Jesus that Bruce Marchiano portrayed. He was a fun loving, lively, energetic Jesus. I bought Bruce Marchiano's book, In the Footsteps of Jesus, and my heart ached inside to do something all the more with urgency which lasted for months. I wrote to him, but was sent a response that he did not need any help but thanked me for my offer and prayers. As the urgency in my heart did not decline, I wrote to Bruce again. I was filled with anticipation which refused to calm. I wrote to him my feelings, taking a chance of sounding ridiculous because I had to act on my faith to show God and myself that I was committed to do His work. This time, I received no reply. Months passed until I finally prayed for God to take away the urgency in my heart if I was not to help Bruce's ministry. When I awoke the following morning, my heart did not have the same strong urgency to help him, but still felt that I was supposed to do *something*. I've always had a feeling that I was

---

8. Matthew - The Gospel According to Matthew. Visual Bible International, Brentwood, TN 37027. Copyright 1994 Visual International.

meant to do something special for God, but ever since I've had my near-death-like-experience, that feeling deep inside grew strong; but what was it! What did God want me to do?

It wasn't until I received the *Onjinjinkta* newsletter in the spring of 2000 that I read about Betty Eadie beginning a publishing company of her own.   She described the book, The Soul's Remembrance, by Roy Mills.   It was about a man who was born without the veil of forgetfulness when he entered his life on Earth.   Only a few weeks earlier, I had speculated about this very thing. I wondered, "Since Jesus is in Heaven and if our resurrection had already taken place,[9] then surely someone could have a memory before coming to Earth.   Wouldn't God want the truth known and permit someone to have their veil removed, at least partially?   There had to be someone in the world with the memory of Heaven because, if I'm correct, all spiritual truth is revealed on Earth from one spectrum to its compliment,

---

9. 2 Timothy 2:18

whether we realize it or not. Since I know that Heaven exists then someone on Earth should remember it. Isn't it peculiar that I found Roy's book at the time I was contemplating about this very thing! Another synchronicity.

I knew immediately that I had to read his story. I had read many books regarding spiritual attributes and I wanted to read all I could find about all the miraculous hidden truths of God's realm. It is written, *"but to this very day, every time the Law of Moses is read, a veil lies over the minds of the hearers."*[10] I wanted to understand the scriptures clearly without the veil.

"Here, then, are two irrevocable acts in which God could not possibly play us false, to give powerful encouragement to us, who have claimed his protection by grasping the hope set before us. That hope we hold. It is like an anchor for our lives, an anchor safe and sure. It enters in through the veil, where Jesus has entered on our behalf as

---

10. 2 Corinthians 3:15

forerunner. "[11] What does this mean? I want to enter through the veil as well.

I ordered Roy Mills' book immediately at my hometown bookstore. I received it on May 17, 2000 and read the first half that same day, and the remainder the following day. I then decided to write to Roy Mills, but feared that he would not respond. Two and a half weeks after I sent my letter, amazingly, I received a phone call from his secretary. She said that Roy was touched by my letter and wanted to talk with me.

Wow! I couldn't believe that he actually contacted me and liked my letter. We set up an appointment to talk on the phone. Roy was very congenial and polite, and I had an 'at-ease' feeling talking with him. He was very calm and answered any of my questions to the best of his ability. I have not found anything that he has told me that could not be supported by scripture in the Bible, or other religious sources. He said he had already decided to be open to talk with anyone who needed his help.

---

11. Hebrews 6:18-20

He understood how I wanted to find someone to support and understand my own experience. There just aren't many people to relate with concerning spiritual matters. I needed to find someone to actually talk with, who *experienced* similar spiritual encounters.

I asked him some bizarre questions that I wouldn't ask anyone else and was pleased that he took no offense with me. Over time we talked more and became friends. I told Roy about my experience, and that I had written my account down on paper. He asked me to send it to him. After he read my account, (which was then only about 10,000 words), he sent it back to me and encouraged me to write a book. I didn't think I had enough to say at that point in my life to write an entire book. What else should I write about? I knew in my heart that God really did want me to share my story but I needed much more information if I were to write an entire book. I never attempted this before, but then within a few weeks, ideas poured into my mind which inspired me to write. My desire to write my own book took over the urgent yearning I've had in my heart. My mind poured forth with words as I began writing everything that flowed out with ease.

I know that I was called by God to write about my personal account because I've connected to my life mission which I'll expand on in a later chapter. For the first time in my life, I feel as though I've found my calling for I have had so much fun writing my book. I had previously tested the water years earlier when I told a few people about my visit with God. I knew some people would have difficulty believing me, but I am more concerned with telling the truth. I could not stand to hold back my story knowing that it could help some people to embrace our spiritual nature and to draw closer to God.

I realized that many people are not enthusiastic about searching for God because they do not know that it is possible. They haven't experienced what's there to discover yet. Some people are content with only going to church on

Sunday, but they don't realize that God truly is there to be found! I wouldn't trade my experience of meeting Him face to face in the spirit world for anything or anyone in the entire world. Not a day goes by that I don't think about it and every day of my life is full of hope of seeing Him again. I thrive in the joy of serving God in any way my life is able to give Him glory. I don't want to do anything to confuse anyone, but if it is possible for me to help others through my testimony, then it is worth my effort of sharing it. As I focus on the day I will return to Him again I am given strength and encouragement.

"To Him who has power to make your standing sure, according to the Gospel I brought you and the proclamation of Jesus Christ, according to the revelation of that divine secret kept in silence for long ages but now disclosed, and through prophetic scriptures by eternal God's command made known to all nations to bring them to faith and obedience - to God who alone is wise, through Jesus Christ, be glory for endless ages!

Amen. "[12]

God wants the truth known to all people and we are literally called by God to be His witness. He wants everyone around the world to have faith and obedience to God, but don't let the word 'obedience' scare you. It's not a strict, cold or brutal obedience at all. It's an obedience of wanting to dedicate our lives to the cause of love. Everything is motivated by love when we are moved by the spirit. Christ was sent to proclaim the Gospel (Good News) which did not rely on the world's wisdom. His message was love. Through all the world's ways of strength, power and wisdom, they failed to find God with the wisdom of men. Those who had faith in the power of God had hope to find the Truth.[13] I truly believe that the ways of God, which in the world's opinion seem silly, are wiser than the wisdom of men.

I understand that the intent of religion was to bring people to God in faith, trust and love. Along

---

12. Romans 16:25-27

13. 1 Corinthians 1:17-31

the way, through its development, the 'yeast of the Pharisees' was sifted through with selfish pride and greed. Prophets and messengers of God came to bring understanding to all people in all nations as they needed guidance to place them back onto the righteous path of love. Unfortunately, people tried to own religion and fought over which religion was correct and which were wrong. Eventually religion was used as a barrier of division among men instead of binding men back to God in love and peace. Thus, people were separated into sects which continued to divide with each new messenger or difference of interpretation. They couldn't see that all messengers came from the same one God and delivered the same core message in which people to this day have difficulty comprehending. They weren't sent to start a new religion or to abolish another religion, but to further explain what was already given that the people didn't understand.

Any person, wherever they live and regardless of religious preference, has the opportunity to find God. God does not bar anyone from His kingdom. It is men who place obstacles and barriers between us and God. If you don't want to find God then you may not. But I give my testimony that God is to be found by a sincere seeker of truth.

Indeed, God's knowledge is immense and unfathomable for our limited bodies to contain! Learning comes by increments. Can a student pass his test on the first day of class just because he was just handed his textbook? Surely people can comprehend that we need to read and study the contents to evolve in our understanding. And while some people advance, others do not, thus we need many teachers to instruct the course.

"Can you not see that while there is jealousy and strife among you, you are living on the purely human level of your lower nature? When one says, 'I am Paul's man', and another, 'I am for Apollos', are you not all too human? After all, what is Apollos? What is Paul? We are simply God's agents in bringing you to the faith." [Does this ring a bell about the different religions around the

world? When one says, 'I am Catholic', and another, 'I am Baptist/Jewish/Muslim/etc.', are you not all too human?] *"Each of us performed the task which the Lord allotted to him: I planted the seed, and Apollos watered it; but God made it grow. Thus it is not the gardeners* [or the various prophets] *with their planting and watering who count, but God, who makes it grow. Whether they plant or water, they work as a team, though each will get his own pay for his own labour. We are God's fellow-workers; and you are God's garden."*[14]

Again, we are God's garden. This is a parable which is still greatly misunderstood. Each variation of flowers represents nations and their unique differences of culture and religion. There are many flowers in each variety, but all flowers take their nourishment from the same Earth. They are all flowers: daisy, lily, rose, violets, etc. each with their own designated beauty, color, shape and

---

14. 1 Corinthians 3:3-9

fragrance. They all need sunlight, water and air - the beginning foundation to sustain life within the soil.

Controlling people try so hard to manipulate and control other people until each culture and religion is conformed into a single cookie-cutter form. This is like transforming each diverse flower into being just a bouquet of roses. Although roses are beautiful by themselves, they also have thorns. People don't realize that this can never be done unless we destroy all flowers that are not roses. Since each culture and religion has its own beauty and purpose, we fight to keep our flower alive.

God created the beauty of a grand bouquet of all species of flowers. Likewise, we are all of one family of humankind - one humanity - displaying our own unique beauty and talents, flourishing on the same planet. We were not created as clones of one another, but with diverse colors of skin, eyes and hair. Can't we learn from nature's parables? It is our own prejudice against each other and our need to overpower and control others which nurtures the negative emotions and actions of hatred and fear amongst our differences. If we will look beyond ourselves, we can share this same planet and enjoy the beauty of diversity. God created all things in diversity. Who are we to destroy it?

Seven
Finding the Root

"Out of darkness let light shine"
2 Corinthians 4:5

After my encounter in the Light with God, I started searching and reading numerous spiritual books and ancient religious documents. I wanted to find any reference that described any of my experiences in any form of religion. I wanted to know more about our spiritual life than what was expounded on in the Bible and church. I wanted to find reference to the truths which had been revealed to me in spirit, but were not taught in depth by the clergy. Religious books are supposed to be about God's guidance so there has to be more explanations written down somewhere.

One day in 1991, I made an appointment to

share with the new minister of my church about my experience in Heaven because the Bible guides us to give testimony about God and not hide it under a bushel. His profession is about God, so I assumed that he would be interested in my testimony. I could tell the moment that I opened my mouth that this minister was not open to my experience. Our church's previous minister passed away and this new minister doesn't know anything about me. I could see and sense the rejection in his eyes and by his demeanor. From that point on I felt that this minister began antagonizing me until my family left that church. How can this be? I had dedicated my life to the church for years, ever since I became pregnant with my son because I wanted to bring him up in the church. Everything that I did in that church was done with love and dedication which was my plumb line to joy. How or why would this church minister betray my trust and reject my spiritual testimony?

This is the moment when my eyes were opened wide to examine the clergy that was instilled in Christians to trust. I questioned that if the leaders of the church cannot embrace honest spiritual truth, then why are they preaching about the Holy Spirit, heaven and God? I strongly felt that if the minister of my church doesn't acknowledge or embrace the truth, then he shouldn't be in that business. I can read the Bible for myself. I don't need him to just regurgitate what it says. I need a minister who can go beyond that and to help me to better understand all of the spiritual things that I had experienced throughout my life. I needed support and understanding. Isn't this one of the duties of a minister? Aren't they supposed to be know-ledgeable about the spirit realm, at least to be able to direct us toward those who have more experience with it? I'll just have to keep searching on my own since he has no assistance to offer me.

As I searched through scriptures I wondered why there were some discrepancies between what some clergy teach from the scriptures found in the Bible? The Bible itself states; *"(whether in the body or out of it, I do not know - God knows) was caught up as far as the third heaven . . . into paradise."*[15] Obviously, this state of being *in the body* or *out of the body* was possible and accepted by the one who wrote this scripture so why is it frowned upon and rejected by some leaders of the church if it happens today? I know that there is much, much more than I was told by the church leaders. But, why doesn't the clergy teach more about these spiritual possibilities? Why do some religious clerics take it upon themselves to 'speak in the name of the Lord' only to reject or ridicule true spiritual testimonies that happen in modern times? Do they believe that God cannot or will not ever reveal Himself to us? But what about the scripture that says that God does? What gives them the right to control or limit what people are to believe or experience regarding the things of the spirit? What gives the church leaders the right to act as religious despots when many of them hadn't even experienced spiritual things for themselves? Haven't the modern day religious leaders learned

---

15. 2 Corinthians 12:1-3

from the mistakes of the past leaders that it was wrong to persecute and murder God's prophets, messengers and servants? Why do these clerics, who were not chosen by God, choose on their own to become priests and ministers? Why do they persecute or stigmatize those who testify in truth of their own personal spiritual experiences 'as if' there is no spirit? Isn't that the point of ministry?

I can understand that a person who has never encountered anything spiritual may doubt and mock the things of the spirit, but why then would any of them choose to become involved with religion if they don't honestly believe in the spirit? What is religion without the things of the spirit but an empty teaching of hypocrisy! Now I felt orphaned by a church that felt like a fraud! This gives me no pleasure to discover that I had been duped by people who should not have been leaders in the church. If I sincerely seek the truth then I must stick with the evidence that I find. I now felt that I had to be on my own to seek wherever my journey takes me.

I searched through the Bible and knew that there must be more books to explain more about my unanswered questions. I began reading the Apocrypha, the Book of Enoch, the Lost Books of the Bible and the Forgotten Books of Eden, and many others. Then I was led to find the Dead Sea Scrolls that were found in the Qumran. They were written around the time when the Bible was written, but were sealed in clay jars to be forgotten until 1947 when a Bedouin shepherd boy found them. This was a very significant find because these scrolls are dated earlier by about 1,000 years than any previously known copy of the Old Testament. They included scrolls or fragments of all the books of the Old Testament (except for the book of Esther), the Apocrypha, and special writings of the Dead Sea sect. I found a cache of so many more books to read and study.

A couple years earlier, in 1945, the scrolls of the Nag Hammadi Library were found, except they were deciphered after the Dead Sea Scrolls. They were composed by early Christians and buried around 400 C.E. (Even after reading the scrolls from the Qumran, I still felt confused and perturbed by the difficulty in reading much of them due to the tremendous amount of information that had deteriorated. I couldn't come to any further conclusions, but only possibilities.) They did help me to expand my thoughts.

This inspired me to wonder just how did the Bible become what it is today? Who determined which books to include and which books to keep out? I wanted to know what Constantine and the Council of Nicaea decided to keep out of the Bible when they decided to canonize it in the year 325 C.E. How could I find which religious manuscripts were available at that time and how did they determine which were legitimate? There have always been much controversy and misunderstandings about religion. There must be a reason why it developed the way it did. Constantine had a vital role in spreading Christianity and I am directed to accept his views and the views of more than 300 bishops of that era. But what was the mind set of that era and of those men?

The history of that era should be reviewed and not forgotten, but it is not my intent to give in detail its violence, struggle, downfalls and triumphs, for which other books give excellent reference of that account. I listed the books where I found the following information in the *Bibliography and Additional Reading* section of this book.

During the 3rd Century C.E., seventy inspired scholars translated the Hebrew canon into Greek. They named this translation the Septuagint (Latin for 70). It was from this Greek translation, which was available to be read and shared at a time when only a quarter of the population was literate. Most people had to hope and trust that their church leaders were knowledgeable and honest about scripture.

Before Constantine became the emperor, he served under Diocletian in Egypt in 296 C.E. Persecution of the Christians began after a meeting in the church Nicomedia on February 23, 303 C.E. at the feast of Terminalia. The next day a decree was enforced, requiring all Christians to return to their forefather's religion or lose their civic rights. The people rebelled because this would return some freed people back into slavery. Starting with the clergy, those who refused were arrested, imprisoned, and compelled to either sacrifice to the Emperor or suffer death. Later, all Christians were forced into the same treatment. Some abandoned and recanted their faith under torture which suited the authorities because they were mainly determined to break their allegiance to God. But instead of the decline of Christianity, it continued to spread.

Following these events, Constantine fought several battles leading up to the last when he was shown a miraculous sign in the noonday sky of the cross and with it the words: 'By this conquer!' He fashioned a flag with the Chi-Rho emblem, being half pagan and half Christian, and went into battle against Maxentius at the Milvian Bridge. He defeated them and became the emperor of the Western Roman Empire, giving the credit of his victory to his vision of the cross. Constantine the Great (Flavius Valerius Aurelius Constantinus) was tolerant of the pagan cults before he saw the old gods of Rome losing their popularity because so many people were turning to Christianity. Constantine wanted to head a universal empire and wanted to choose a religion that would bind people together under his rule. He saw the strength in the followers of Christianity as it increasingly spread in spite of persecutions and threats. As a result, he adopted the Christian religion officially on October 28, 312 C.E. Unfortunately, this decision did not bind all people together in peace. Fighting and arguing still continued.

Constantine devoted himself to correcting the tyrant abuses in the administration of the laws. He chastised the barbarians from the invasions of the Goths and other tribal groups. He also gathered in Milan in 313 C.E. to discuss and place all religions on a par. He was in favor of the churches and exempted them from taxation, implemented gifts and grain allowances to widows and those who were in service to the church.

Around 318 C.E., there began a great argument upheaval when Arius (Arianism) viewed his opinions of the Trinity. This controversy rapidly spread throughout the Church until it stirred up enough attention to prompt Constantine to gather more than 300 bishops in Nicaea (325 C.E.) to settle the dispute and then they formulated a document of their beliefs which they named the Nicene Creed. Although they adopted Athanasians' and Origens' point of view, the majority of the people were in favor or Arius' and Tertullians's views. Constantine's overruling was an extremely daring, brazen act committed by an autocrat in disregard and defiance of the vast majority of his subjects which turned out to have been a rash mistake. He was forced to reopen the debate for further discussion and the arguments continued because it could not be settled by an appeal to scripture and tradition. Both views could find support, and so a second council was summoned at Constantinople and the Nicene Creed was modified in 381 C.E.

So if 300 bishops debated and fiercely argued for more than six decades about the correct understanding of the scriptures, how can anyone be sure that their decisions were right and infallible? It wasn't as if they were all in agreement, especially when they were bribed by Constantine to follow his ruling or be excommunicated from the Church if they continued to oppose him. So then the understanding of the scriptures was not so clear to them and there was coercion involved to accept one view and to reject another. This is not what I was told about the beginnings of Christianity through the church! We were taught that the church was infallible and that we should not question the authorities. Seems as though we were being manipulated through brainwashing. Ever since I was a young child, I could sense that this world was forcing us to conform to its way of thinking, but at the expense of denying the truth. The more I research, the more I find evidence.

If the scriptures were so clear, then why do evangelists differ about the message even today? I am extremely indebted beyond words to the efforts of these strongly dedicated people in whom their debates gave a footing to the permanent endurance of the documents within the Bible today, but what about the manuscripts that were rejected? Why were they withheld? Are there ideas that we need to reexamine that the people of that time didn't embrace? Could we or should we embrace it today? Perhaps some truth was overlooked or rejected from the very beginning.

I wonder how Socrates would have thought about the conclusion of these councils? I feel that he wouldn't force anyone to conform to a set standard, especially when there continued to be varying opinions. How do we know without a doubt what is the truth, unless it is revealed to us by God or proven beyond a doubt? The intent of canonizing the Bible was to distinguish which doctrines were divinely inspired, but what if they made some mistakes of judgment?

The lesson I've learned is that we should not judge anyone or assume anything without witnessing the truth for ourselves or receiving personal revelations from God. It is an injustice to stifle the truth just because it doesn't conform to our beliefs. Our beliefs could be in error. I don't like censorship about spiritual things because not all people understand it in quite the same way.

People throughout history wanted something tangibly dependable that they could comprehend. Even throughout the various religions today, people try to regulate the scriptures and control its guidance by human understanding. Human error is inevitable when the truth of God is perceived to be confined in a neat package of their own human standards. By insisting their human interpretations are complete and faultless, they are actually shutting the truth out because God cannot be bound by human conditions. It doesn't dawn on them that God is unfathomable to the mortal mind. People must transcend the mortal mind and discover their higher self for the scriptures to come to life. There must be freedom for truth to reveal itself and freedom is boundless in the spirit. All things are possible through God.

It is pointless to argue about theologies for what is true to one person may be perceived or experienced differently by infinite variations and yet there is the straight narrow path of God's divine intention that we humans can't quite grasp. There is a difference between what each person believes from what is true and faultless. The truth, one can only say, is witnessed through the spirit. The search of truth is an ongoing journey which is revealed through our lives as we go deeper and deeper into an awakened state of mind.

The truth of God is eternal, and nothing changes Him; only our perceptions change as we become more knowledgeable. The Gospels are records of events, not concrete definitions of what or who God is. That's why God said, **"I AM WHO I AM."**[16]   Only God can reveal to us who He is. And that is why we are His witnesses.[17]   *"My*

---

16. Exodus 3:14 (from the *Hebrew Greek Word Study Bible*, Cambridge University Press, New York, 1970.)

17. John 15:27

witnesses, says the LORD, are you, my servants, you whom I have chosen to know me and put your faith in me and understand that I am He. Before me there was no god fashioned nor ever shall be after me."[18] So there you have it. God's witnesses are those people to whom God chooses to know Him.

Likewise, to argue about who Jesus is, in the same light of truth, is pointless to define. The truth reveals itself in its own time, in its own way. People argue over religious belief, yet who is right when we each are such strong adherents to our own belief? It's a quandary of beliefs! This is why I feel that it is good to preserve all scriptures for the information they hold and for the events they tell, but then let alone any speculative conclusions until the answer is revealed through divine testimony. Dictating the theology about religion is pointless when people cannot distinguish the truth without a doubt from all points of view. Perhaps that's why religious battles and wars continue onward today. The full truth still wants to be known and so

---

18. Isaiah 43:10

struggles and pulls against the fixed mindset that was formed by earthly opinions of doctrines and commandments of men. Jesus said, *"This people pays me lip-service, but their heart is far from me; their worship of me is in vain, for they teach as doctrines the commandments of men."*[19] Jesus warned us, *"Be on your guard against the leaven of the Pharisees and Sadducees."*[20] It seems to me that this is still a problem today in almost any religion.

Jesus said, *"I did not come to abolish [the Law nor the prophets], but to complete [them],"*[21] and also said of the church leaders, *"Do what they tell you; pay attention to their words. But do not follow their practice; for they say one thing and do another."*[22] This clearly indicates the problem of men's comprehension of the scriptures by the

---

19. Matthew 15:8

20. Matthew 16:6

21. Matthew 5:17

22. Matthew 23:3

authorities.

This roused me to want to know what was in their scriptures that they had in the time of Jesus' life on Earth. I would need to research and find which actual Laws they had before the Bible was constructed and canonized as it is today. Through research, this is what I found...

The Hebrew Bible was regarded as the work of the Great Assembly associated with Ezra in the latter part of the 5th Century B.C. It consisted of the *Torah*, *Neviim*, and the *Ketuvim*:

1. The *Torah* contained the five books attributed to Moses, which included Genesis, Exodus, Leviticus, Numbers, and Deuteronomy. They were canonized in the 4th Century B.C. to the middle of the 5th Century B.C.

2. The *Neviim* consisted of the former prophets (Joshua, Judges, 1 & 2 Samuel, 1 & 2 Kings), later prophets (Isaiah, Jeremiah, and Ezekiel), and the 12 minor prophets (Hosea, Joel,

Amos, Obadiah, Jonah, Micah, Nahum, Habakkuk, Zephaniah, Haggai, Zechariah, and Malachi). They were canonized about 400 B.C.

3. The *Ketuvim* were the writings of Ruth, 1 & 2 Chronicles, Ezra, Nehemiah, Esther, Job, Psalms, Proverbs, Ecclesiastes, Song of Songs, Lamentations and Daniel. They were canonized around 90 C.E.

Much is now known about the Hebrew texts from which the ancient versions were made, especially because of the Hebrew scrolls found in the Qumran (the Dead Sea Scrolls). Judaism is based mainly on the Hebrew canon and the Talmud. The Talmud is a collection of Jewish oral laws (Mishnah) and commentaries of the rabbis (Gamara). The Protestant churches generally adopted the Hebrew canon for the Old Testament but the Talmud was kept to the Jewish faith because it was not written down until about 200 C.E. Thus their practices and ceremonies reflected their beliefs according to the laws and commentaries of their rabbis.

Since I am concerned with the covenant received directly from Moses, I wanted to know what was also in the Mishnah. Exodus 34:1 says, *"The LORD said to Moses, ''Cut two stone tablets like the first, and I will write on the tablets the words which were on the first tablets, which you broke in pieces.'"* Then in verse 27-28: *"The LORD said to Moses, 'Write these words down, because the covenant I make with you and with Israel is in these words! So Moses stayed there with the LORD forty days and forty nights, neither eating nor drinking, and wrote down the words of the covenant - the Ten Words, on the tablets."*

The LORD replaced the first tablets with the same words, then asked Moses to write. The Ten Commandments were the principle covenants from which the entire Law of Moses derived. The 'words of the covenant' were isolated into 613 separate commandments by ancient rabbis. I would like to read the laws as they originally came from God without human interpretation so that people would be able to reflect on them today from the original source devoid of any human interpolation. As I researched the commentaries in search of the 613 separate commandments, I had learned of disagreements between the Pharisaic sages and the Sadducees who rejected the oral tradition. I also found that the deeper one digs into the Jewish books, the more complicated and intricate they become with their in-depth hidden meaning and concepts. It would be interesting to find the genuine 'words of the covenant' before they were deciphered into commentaries and oral laws (Mishnah), especially when Jesus warned us that men teach as doctrines the commandments of men.

Jesus said, *"Unless you show yourselves far better men than the Pharisees and the doctors of the law, you can never enter the kingdom of Heaven."*[23] He also said, *"Alas for you, lawyers and Pharisees, hypocrites! You clean the outside of the cup and dish, which you have filled inside by robbery and*

---

23. Matthew 5:20

self-indulgence! Blind Pharisee! Clean the inside of the cup first; then the outside will be clean also." This reminds me of the Christian ministry today as well as others, although we can't assume that all Pharisees, (religious leaders) are all the same. Religion seems to always be controlled by people of which some things are understood and some are not.

Jesus was disgusted with their murdering and self-seeking pride. He explained that God had sent prophets, sages, and teachers to help them understand. They had the correct Laws, but developed self-important attitudes and traditions that reflected the carnal (outside) flesh. If they understood that the Laws were referring to the inner spirit, then they should have developed generosity, peace-making, love and forgiveness. Instead they grew self-pride, war, hate, stinginess, and crime.[24] They had chosen to follow through the opposing path away from God instead of the righteous path which would bind them to God. In desperation, Jesus admonished them because they would not see.

---

24. Matthew 23:1-39

Through his warnings, he was trying to open their eyes, not to condemn them, but to help them. It was their choice to either heed the warning or to reject it. Unfortunately, their iniquities formed a barrier between them and God.[25]

I can see the same self-pride, prejudice, war, hate and crime sifted throughout all religions as each one rejects and condemns the other. Many religious leaders instill fear and hatred towards different people. We all seem to reflect each other like a chameleon of different colors and yet we can't see our own faults. We are still struggling to value all humans as members of the human race. Each adherent of religion doesn't see the other religions as fellow followers of the Faith, but as competition and enemies to conquer.

Would our Father God that I met in Heaven create human beings to kill each other off? I can't even conceive of it! The story of Cain murdering his brother Abel revealed a God who was not pleased with murder. Didn't God give us free will?

---

25. Isaiah 59:2

Don't we have a right to choose our own course of religion without coercion? Why then, do we go to war over religion? How can God want us to condemn each other to death if He is loving, compassionate and merciful? This tells me that people of all religions had continued to misunderstand, at least in part, the message of God. We all need to get back on track and rethink the message and watch our motives.

Eight
Contemplating Scripture

"[God] has caused his light to shine within
us, to give the light of revelation."
2 Corinthians 4:6

Now that I am being drawn into contemplating scripture with the knowledge from my
spiritual experiences, I'm seeing and understanding
it with new vision. Scripture feels more clear to me
and more sure and I can see where so many people
have made assumptions that were not on track.
They have gone astray without realizing it. All of
the wars that were fought in the name of God was
not necessary. So much pain, agony and death! Is
there anyone who is willing to heed warnings so
that we may turn this world around toward peace?
Who will listen?

Scripture states that God made a covenant with Abraham that *"all the families of the earth shall find blessing . . . by turning every one of you from your wicked ways."*[26] How will we find peace as long as we fight to dominate and control over the will of others? Until the human race is living in righteousness with faith and obedience in God, (instead of obedience to despotic, misguided leaders set on war), we must turn our heart, mind, and strength back into studying scripture with freedom and an open heart to allow God's power to give us revelation. When the world is blessed and reflects mostly goodness, then that will be a sign that we know and understand the ways of God. In life, we reap what we sow. We all want to reap a peaceful world of love and kindness but we don't sow the seeds of righteousness. Instead, in ignorance we sow seeds of fear, prejudice, bigotry, greed and hate.

Religious bigotry must be ignorance most assuredly for it certainly does not bring peace.

---

26. Acts 3:26 and Genesis 18:18-20

People gave their trust to men who claimed to understand the scriptures as they themselves were taught by men who argued about the correct understanding. Some leaders were on the right track, but if all religious leaders understand the scriptures as they should be understood, then why do so many sects disagree with one another when they study the same doctrines? How can there be so many variations of interpretations if they weren't interpreted by men's understanding? Surely some are in error, but which ones? How can we distinguish the just pious leaders from the unjust errant leaders who are leading people away from God? How many people actually find God? mHmmm, so why should any man dictate and control our devotion of God? How can our devotion be sincere from the heart if it is forced on us? Shouldn't we focus directly on God (who is the source of divine scripture) to guide us? Please don't doubt this possibility.

"Only by declaring the truth openly do we recommend ourselves, and then it is to the common

conscience of our fellowmen and in the sight of God. . . . For the same God who said, 'Out of darkness let light shine', has caused his light to shine within us, to give the light of revelation - the revelation of the glory of God in the face of Jesus Christ."[27] Therefore, the light of revelation is the key to finding the truth about God's true way.

I am happy to inform that as I've started to study more Jewish doctrines that were not included in the Old Testament, I've found that their scriptures do tell of some of the spiritual mysteries that I have had. They hope for the revealing of the image of a man on a throne, which is the vision of the Shi'ur Komah.[28] This is hidden from the sight of every creature, and concealed from the ministering angels. 'The Glory' is referred as being the guf ha-Shekhinah, 'the body of the Divine Presence.' This sounds like my (NDLE) experience of being in the presence of God in Heaven! All along, there were documents in other religious sects

---

27. 2 Corinthians 4:2-6

28. Scholem, Gershom. Kabbalah. page 16

that reveal these mysteries! How unfair of religious leaders not to encourage us to find these hidden treasures in other doctrines. Instead, we are taught through their ignorance of the spirit, through their bigotry and prejudice of other doctrines!

There is so much more to learn about God and life than what I had been told in my own brand of religion. How dare the religious leaders keep me from the truth! But it's because they don't know any better. They need someone to point them in the right direction, but how may anyone get through to them? We have to have religious freedom to grow in understanding and learn step by step the mysteries of our world and God. It is unjust to stifle and muzzle the truth. Doing so will only perpetuate the same problems. No wonder religious battles rage on! The Truth is still waiting to be known. We must search in freedom to allow the light of revelation to shine within us.

I realize now that scripture can't help us grow and mature with the spirit if we don't understand its concept in the right light. Contrary to the correct intentions of the scriptures, its lessons are obscure to those minds which have not evolved along virtuous spiritual lessons and may even be misused for the wrong intentions. This is why scripture guides; *"to this very day, every time the Law of Moses is read, a veil lies over the minds of the hearers."*[29]

For example, through my near-death-like experience, when I realized that my spirit was separated from my physical body, I then realized that our body is our cage or container which binds us to the Earth. Scripture explains: *"We groan indeed, we who are enclosed within this earthly frame; we are oppressed because we do not want to have the old body stripped off. Rather our desire is to have the new body put on over it, so that our mortal part may be absorbed into life immortal. God himself has shaped us for this very end; and as a pledge of it he has given us the Spirit."*[30]

This concept was misunderstood and

---

29. 2 Corinthians 3:15

30. 2 Corinthians 5:4-5

exasperated one of the cruel punishments of the wicked carnal mind set. The persecutors of the early Christians filleted people alive or sewed them inside animal skins to be eaten alive by tigers and wild animals. In ignorance, they were ridiculing, mocking, and taunting the Christians because the persecutors' mind was veiled of revelation of its proper meaning and understanding. They could not conceive of the truth of this scripture because they had not *experienced* it for themselves. Therefore, they wouldn't even attempt to understand the scriptures with its true meaning. They were torturing innocent Christians because of their own spiritual blindness.

In their mind, they thought that they were proving that the Christians were liars by filleting their skin open only to reveal, in their worldly understanding, that the body was not two bodies, but one. But exposing this human understanding of the scriptures in effect did not thwart the growth of Christianity, but rather grew stronger in faith. The followers of Christ were willing to die from cruel, insidious crimes because they believed the correct spiritual intent of the scriptures. They understood that there is a spiritual body and a physical body.

Such is the dilemma between those people who have experienced and/or understood spiritual things beyond those who have not. The Spirit renews us inwardly and helps us to grow in understanding and to become righteous. We are immortal beings without the flesh, but if the Holy Spirit is not transforming us for the better, then we are not maturing through the life lessons that were orchestrated to guide us to become our fullest potential. How can people grow in spiritual knowledge and reach their highest potential without examples and testimonies from others who have evolved in understanding and who have witnessed these true possibilities?

I can now understand how many things written in the scriptures could be misunderstood. The intent of tithing, offerings for sin, and sacrifice could have been misused and were attributed to the flesh instead of the spirit:

131

Tithing

A) Tithing was not intended to take money away from the citizens to give to the Pharisees and Sadducees, (our religious leaders) to pamper and spoil them in riches. It was taught to help the people in need, to lift them up and out of their deprivation and poverty. It's an act of love and charity to help those who are desperately in need of the basic necessities. The religious leaders were included because they devoted their lives to teach the ways of God and had very little time to work elsewhere to support themselves. A part of the tithe was to support the leaders of the synagogues, but it was also to be used for others who needed assistance. But while the Pharisees and Sadducees were dressed in fine robes, there were so many orphans and widows suffering in the streets. This was what Jesus was referring to when he said that the Pharisees were blind guides and filled with robbery, self-indulgence and greed. They were already taken care of through tithing, but they wanted more. They tilted the balance in their favor and became greedy.

There are many religious leaders today, in any religious faith, who are in the ministry for the fame, power, glory and riches. And still to this day, we have so many poor and homeless people suffering in our societies. When I see so many TV evangelists begging for money when they live such luxurious lifestyles, I have to wonder about their motives as well. This is the first indication for me to stay away from them because their motivation and focus was not truly God-centered. I can't see how any religious leader can splurge so fluidly on self indulgences and relish in their wealth without at least trying to help some of the many hungry and homeless people who are in desperate need and despair.

Offerings for sin

B) Offerings for sin was not necessarily to be in material gifts or money (depending on the crime). The intent was to undo the sin with the opposing force to nullify or counteract the incorrect offense. If someone steals, then they should give of something in equal balance of the offense. This was the meaning for an eye for an eye, and a tooth for a tooth. It did not mean to do wrong for wrong, but to counteract wrong with good with its equal opposite side of the pole: left to right and top to bottom.

I have a hunch that Egyptians were buried with treasure to offer payment for their sins in the afterlife. The more accepted understanding was that the Egyptians were buried with treasures for their own pleasure in their afterlife. In either case, their treasures lie dormant in dust and deterioration. God did not take their material treasures, nor did the dead take it with them in the spiritual realm. God was not wanting 'things' for payment of sins.[31] He wanted a contrite heart.

If someone murders (puts to an end a life that was), then the opposite force would be restoring life (returning the life that was). But since man cannot restore life, God designed Christ to

---

31. Ezekiel 7:19

counteract the offense of our sins of murder. Christ brings to life what men put to death. Jesus was sent to do this job for all humanity. That is why He could raise the dead! He was, and still is, the life-giving vessel. We need to emulate Christ in our lives - so that we may have hope of a resurrection like his in Glory.

Sacrifice

C) Sacrifice was not intended to mean to kill the fleshly body of innocent animals or humans as a payment to God for our sins. The fleshly sacrifices were a symbol of its true intent to teach us the ways of the spirit which the people didn't understand at that time. The intent is to willingly sacrifice our lives to serve others through pure intentions. We need to place our own selfish interests behind to focus on the well being of others. The fleshly body symbolizes the separation or outer life away from God. We are to remove our focus of the outer life of living for 'self' and instead, give one's life to God. This does not mean that we are to hate or kill our body of flesh, but to stop living for only our own selfish ambitions without regard to others. The intent was to bring us back in alignment with God.

This is how Jesus became the sacrifice for all. *"It is God's way of <u>righting wrong</u> effective through faith in Christ for all who have such faith – all, without distinction. For all alike have sinned, and are deprived of the divine splendour, and all are justified by God's free grace alone, through his act of liberation in the person of Christ Jesus. For God designed him to be the means of expiating sin by his sacrificial death, effective through faith."*[32] God desires mercy, not sacrifice of the flesh. Christ's sacrifice is a spiritual sacrifice. His whole life was focused on helping others, even unto death.

This is why God designed Christ to counteract the sins of violence, hatred and murder, that we are guilty of committing. This is proof that God loves us. In light of Christ, we are trusting God to blot out our sins, renew our spirits, and

---

32. Romans 3:21-25

restore life to the dead. Without this hope and faith, we are denying the purpose and effect of God's power to save us from ourselves. Without the revelation and the manifestation of Christ in our world, humans would have no awareness or visual demonstration of God's love and salvation. We could not or would not understand how to live righteously before God without an example to follow. In flesh we are not perfect but through the power of the Holy Spirit, we have hope when we place our faith and trust in the power of Christ who is the mercy and grace of God our Father. Without Christ, His Word wouldn't have been manifested into our world to show us a living example of sacrifice that demonstrates God's forgiveness and unending love for us. The Light must penetrate into the human mind to enlighten us. Without this illuminating Light, we will stay in a perpetual state of darkness of the human mindset and not evolve in spirit as we should. Christ is the vessel sent down to Earth to manifest God's essence of love and eternal life. Death is already conquered! Death is really an illusion because our physical eyes are veiled from seeing the spirit.

God emanates His essence into our world to reveal His ways. This act of mercy and grace of forgiveness was emanated down for the sins of the whole world, for all people. This emanation was manifested into Christ so that we may perceive God's love. No one would live a perfect life so there needed to be a way to show forgiveness and to show the way of God's highest goal for us. No one could obtain perfection because no one was perfect, nor did we know what perfection was. So Christ became the living example of His Word. So awesome!

"His purpose in dying for all was that men, while still in life, should cease to live for themselves, [put to death your selfish greed] *and should live for him who for their sake died and was raised to life. With us therefore worldly standards have ceased to count in our estimate of any man. − When anyone is united to Christ, there is a new world; the old order has gone, and a new order has*

already begun."[33]

God is concerned with nurturing our innermost spiritual being which is immortal. Our physical bodies will rot away as a corpse turns to dust, and we will be left without the flesh only to be set free from our bondage to this Earth. After we leave the Earth, God places our soul where He chooses to place us.

"But, you may ask, how are the dead raised? In what kind of body? How foolish! The seed you sow does not come to life unless it has first died; and what you sow is not the body that shall be, but a naked grain, [without the fleshly body] perhaps of wheat, or of some other kind; and God clothes it with the body of his choice, each seed with its own particular body. All flesh is not the same flesh: there is flesh of men, flesh of beasts, of birds, and of fishes – all different. There are Heavenly bodies and earthly bodies; and the splendour of the Heavenly bodies is one thing, the splendour of the earthly, another. The sun has a splendour of its

---

33. 2 Corinthians 5:15-17

own, the moon another splendour, and the stars another, for star differs from star in brightness. So it is with the resurrection of the dead. What is sown in the earth as a perishable thing is raised imperishable. Sown in humiliation, it is raised in glory; sown in weakness, it is raised in power; sown as an animal body, it is raised as a <u>spiritual body</u>.[34]

Our life on Earth is only a small span of years compared to eternity. It is a testing ground to act out and demonstrate what we are inside. Our lives intertwine with one another to develop our world in which we live. If we are to find the blessings of a peaceful world, then we need to focus on living an upright life of loving kindness. The more that people consciously choose to emulate an upright lifestyle, the more our whole world will be transformed and renewed in peace and brought together into a unity of spirit.

---

34. 1 Corinthians 15:35-44

Nine
Socrates / Jesus Parallel

"Then I heard the voice of the Lord saying,
'Whom shall I send, and who will go for
us?' And I said, 'Here am I; send me!"

Isaiah 6:8-9

My husband studied history and philosophy
in college, and he urged me to read *Plato: The Last
Days of Socrates.* He bought the book for me
because he wanted me to compare the thoughts of
Socrates with what Jesus taught. I let the book sit
on the shelf for months before picking it up. I
thought that philosophy would be beyond my
understanding. But once I started reading, I found
the book fairly easy to read and understand.

Even though Socrates lived from 470 or 469
B.C. until 399 B.C., he had many of the same

141

thought processes as Jesus had. He had no other reference to religion other than the Greek gods of his time, but yet, he believed that our real difficulty in this world was to escape from wickedness, and that after death, man would live eternally in another place.[35] I was impressed with Socrates words: *"No one knows with regard to death whether it is not really the greatest blessing that can happen to a man; but people dread it as though they were certain that it is the greatest evil; and this ignorance, which thinks that it knows what it does not, must surely be ignorance most culpable."*[36]

I began researching more information about Socrates. He spent his life searching for the absolute truth and goodness. He thoroughly investigated an idea and reflected upon further inclinations into as many different possibilities as he could conceive and when he ran out of possibilities, he would ask others for their opinions

---

35. Sections 39a and 40c of *The Apology*, <u>Plato: The Last Days of Socrates</u>

36. Section 29a-b of *The Apology*, <u>Plato: The Last Days of Socrates</u>

to hear what they could come up with to open up even deeper in-depth thought. He was a master at trying to understand 'why' and 'how'. He was determined to seek for true justice, courage, nobility and truth to be able to define the complete essence of words and virtues. He had a true love of truth. Everything had to be justified from all angles before a possible conclusion could be made, but even then, he didn't take anything for granted without the possibility of error in judgment. Unless all of the facts are known, no true conclusion could be made. He never came to a final conclusion since there was always a possibility for unrecognized facts and future analysis.

Since childhood, Socrates was always aware of a divine 'sort of voice' which came to him. He was subject to a divine or supernatural experience.[37] Surely he had found God! I can identify with this!

There are no words developed in our vocabulary nor emotions that we have on Earth to completely describe our Father God. It's just as

_____

37. Section 31d of *The Apology*, <u>Plato: The Last Days of Socrates</u>

life: only the person who has lived his own life and discovered for himself the journey can know what he himself finds. The person who finds God can understand this mystery yet finds it difficult to share with others. What is true to one person may be comprehended differently by another for no one can completely fathom God.

This book is written in truth, but it is through my life. It is not known by another unless they had experienced it in totality. I am the only one who had touched it in all essence. Anything received secondhand, is subject to doubt and skepticism because it is not truly known by another recipient. They cannot fathom what they had not found. A seeker wants to find truth, but cannot know it in its entirety unless he finds it for himself. God can be found by the desire of a sincere seeker. That's why it is written: *'Seek and you will find.'* Each and every person needs to want to find God to be able to find Him. Do not take this light heartedly because it is a difficult journey. It takes strong dedication, perseverance through difficult lessons, many heartfelt prayers, and much in-depth study. In my case, I discovered that I had to *desire* to find God.

Though some skeptics have adamantly concluded that no one can see God, they have shut themselves off from a beautiful and indescribable relationship as I have found, by not seeking God. I know their conclusion is not true because I am a witness of God and dispute their conclusion. They have not found God is all they may truthfully say.

There has been people in the Bible and through modern times who had witnessed God through near-death-experiences and other spiritually transformative experiences. Doesn't the Bible say that Abraham,[38] Jacob,[39] Hagar,[40] and Moses[41] saw God? We can't deny and ignore their testimonies if we insist the Bible is true. Does the Bible not say

---

38. Genesis 17:1 & 2

39. Genesis 28:13 and 32:30

40. Genesis 16:14

41. Exodus 33:11

that God will reveal Himself?[42] I believe that God reveals Himself as He wants to be known by each individual or as each individual needs to experience.

This is why Socrates' way of finding the truth is commendable. We are not to believe something just because 'so and so' said so. Search for the truth for yourself. Don't take anything for granted. Find all the facts, and when you think you've found it, go to another point of view, but don't stop searching until you personally discover the answer. It is my sincere hope that everyone may find God and have a personal relationship with Him. It is through this hidden treasure that life is lived more fully and abundantly with wholeness of being.

Even though Socrates' friends knew him to be the most gentle, righteous and loyal person they've ever known, the law voted by a narrow margin for Socrates to drink hemlock to poison himself to death. The people were afraid of Socrates' influence on young minds, and believed

42. Matthew 11:27 and John 14:21

him to be blasphemous because he believed in an inner soul and eternal life. People were afraid of his different ideas about God, even if he was correct. Socrates didn't force his theory or beliefs on others but encouraged them to seek and inquire deeper.

His friends wanted to break him out of prison, but being strong willed as he was not to do anything wrong, he would not lower his principles to go against the law of his people. He lived what he believed even to the point of death. Socrates was not going to deny the truth that he found to conform to the ways of this world. He said that if the law required for him to die, then so be it. He drank the poison without any hesitation. His death was dumbfounding and immoral to those who knew him. He was a companionable person who liked everyone and didn't threaten or detest others. People gathered around him wherever he went to reflect on the topic of the day.

Jesus also accepted the verdict of religious leaders and the law, even to the point of death. Jesus refused obedience to the ways of this world or to any man or religious leader other than God. Jesus too, was called a blasphemer and yet was the most righteous person any had ever known. People gathered around to be enlightened by Jesus' wisdom and perhaps to witness a miracle. He was received into Jerusalem with palm branches and shouts of hosanna, only to be murdered the following week. What happened to these people that shook their faith and destroyed their moral foundation to seek wisdom and truth? Why was a person's differing viewpoint worth murdering? Why do we fear change when it could help resolve worldly conflicts and may actually lead us to find peace?

Ten
An Awakening Vision
Through the Veil

"We speak of these gifts of God in words
found for us not by
our human wisdom but by the Spirit"
1 Corinthians 2:13

As I continued reading about Socrates as I
sat comfortably in my living room recliner beside
my husband as he watched a program on television,
I turned the page to read near the end of the chapter
Phaedo on August 27, 2000. Instantly, the memory
of reading the same two pages I was about to read
came to my mind from Heaven! I knew without a
doubt the context and thought being conveyed. I
didn't need to read any further because I held in my
mind its ending thoughts! My mind opened up into
a vision/memory of a heightened consciousness into

a new dimension as I received revelation of its continued concept which wasn't completed in the *Phaedo*. I will expound on the understanding that I received in my next book about my spiritual connection with Socrates.

All of these spiritual experiences throughout my life now had a connection and correlated with my entire life. Every lesson, every joy, every sadness and pain was all a part of my life's mission and purpose for God.

Is this what the Bible means when it says to 'find our true self?' I felt as someone recovering from a strong case of amnesia! Suddenly, my life was thrust into a new understanding and concept. Tears welled up in my eyes as I began to envision a truth I had not known before and which renewed my purpose in life. This was the first time, at age 39, that I restored some recollection of memories and events that happened *before* my life on Earth. I felt confused and wonderfully amazed at the same time as I questioned, "What does this mean?" My husband was unaware of what had just taken place in a matter of only a few seconds as I sat beside him on the living room recliner. A few seconds that further transformed my view of life.

The following is the account of my vision which is truly an awesome revelation and a true spiritual awakening into another realm of existence of prebirth memories:

My memory was faint of detailed features, but yet I could recall an awareness of standing with a couple of others in Heaven. We were all dressed in white floor-length robes and discussing some disturbing issues when I remembered that I needed to write a book about certain philosophical thoughts. One of them told me not to worry about that book anymore because it had already been written. This person quickly left toward the left and immediately returned with a book and held it open for me to glance down to read its contents. (The speed of reading was as one who looked at something and instantly knew its contents.) The pages I had read were the two pages I had just turned to in the Phaedo which brought this vision memory to me. I was relieved that the book had already been written by someone else; though I knew that it wasn't completely finished to the concept that was needed to be arrived at. Knowing that if people would contemplate further, they would arrive to an answer to their questions about life, death and God. But people have stumbled, and for the most part, haven't gone far enough in thought and have come to a standstill.

In Heaven, I contemplated and considered how the chapter *Phaedo* could lead people to a certain point, which in turn would lead to another step, and again to another point, and a second step, and finally to understand our soul and why people exist in our world on Earth. The group of us pondered about the problem that people (on Earth) are lost and don't know who they really are nor how to rise above the human barriers which confine spiritual growth. There is a better, richer, fuller destiny and way of life for people to live in Heaven and on Earth.

Over the next few weeks, during contemplation of this memory, more was poured into my consciousness as one feels glimpses and pieces of memory seeping in while suffering from an amnesia state of mind. This time, I saw myself standing with two men in Heaven surrounded by whiteness. My memory doesn't recall clearly any faces because they were blurred. I can only retrieve this event from another place and time from an inside perspective connected with a sense of feeling and emotion.

One man had much authority, but I can't recall who he was. Somehow I feel that he may have been Jesus, or *like* Jesus. This man was discussing a problem with me and another male. I don't know who this other male may have been. The man with great authority was filled with sadness as he divulged to us that some people actually choose not to go to Heaven; though we could not understand why. This was a sad decision that really broke this man's heart. My heart could sense the great concern and compassion he had for the people. He said with a sense of desperation;

"Everything was said and done for people to have the truth if they were encouraged to accept it. What else can we do or say to help them any more to take away their fears and unbelief?"

I felt heartfelt sympathy for him and thought to myself, "How could their concepts, (the people on Earth), be taken to the next level of acceptance of faith? What do I understand that they do not? What's missing from their connection? There is no reason for anybody to fear Heaven, so why would some choose not to come?"

It could only mean that they had ignorance of the truth of Heaven. Something was blocking their path. We were all deeply concerned that people needed guidance and understanding to *want* to go to Heaven when they leave Earth. God truly loves us. If people knew the truth they would look forward with anticipation to see our Lord and Father. *"Then I heard the Lord saying, 'Whom shall I send? Who will go for me?' And I answered, 'Here am I; send me!'*[43]

While I vexed about this concern and tried to explain a method that could be used, I inadvertently volunteered. "It's pretty easy to understand. It's really not as complicated as people make it out to be. I think I can explain it through the concept of positive and negative. My added concept can be a stepping stone for people to come to some further ideas to help them understand life, death, and God." It was done. By expressing a way that I thought could help people, it was accepted as though I had volunteered to personally do it. Gulp! Now I couldn't say no.

Then, my memory flashed to another memory. I saw us study and look into a book on a table of some sort. When I looked into its pages, I saw living scenes, and upon it was the future life that I was preparing to embark upon. *"Run with resolution the race for which we are entered."*[44] We were carefully selecting issues for my life. (I

---

43. Isaiah 6:8-9

44. Hebrews 12:2

155

suppose this book is the 'Book of Life' that Isaiah
4:3 and Philippians 4:3 are talking about.)

I was encouraged to choose some form of
physical impairment that could help me focus on
my life journey on Earth, but of course it first had to
be approved by God. I recall considering different
things to choose from a list. As I considered
different options, I contemplated how each potential
choice would affect my life. This was done very
quickly, but thoroughly, almost instantly as I paused
to examine each choice. My thoughts were clear,
deep and penetrating with a speed which surpasses
the earth's speed of thinking to a snail's pace.
Finally, I pinpointed my decision to have a slight
challenge of poor vision and having to wear glasses.
This was to help me not feel too attached to my
physical appearance and vanity. I did not want to
be perfectly flawless, because I didn't want
anything to detain me from wanting to return back
home to Heaven or to distract me off my course. I
knew that life on Earth could distract me away from
my main mission. There was more meaning into

this idea, but for now I cannot recall what they were.

***

A Miracle

This brings to me an understanding of a miraculous incident that happened to me when I was 22 years old. When my first child was a baby, I desperately wanted to be able to see him clearly without the nuisance of searching for my glasses while nursing him in the middle of the night. I prayed repeatedly for months for God to heal my eyes to let me see without glasses. One night, as I sat in the rocking chair preparing to feed my baby, I noticed that he was clear. I looked around the room, and I could clearly see everything. I searched my face, but my glasses were not on. I was so excited that I awakened my husband to tell him that I could see without my glasses and vibrantly pointed to everything that I clearly saw. He was amazed and shocked.

In the morning when I awoke, I was

disappointed to find my vision was back as it was; I needed my glasses again. We wondered why or how I could see in the middle of the night, but now my blurry vision returned. Several months later, this same thing happened again for only one night. Nevertheless, my poor vision returned once again. How did that happen and why?

Eighteen years later, I came to understand what could be the answer. Roy Mills, an author who also has spiritual memories, became a new friend of mine. He told me that before we came to Earth, we agreed upon certain conditions or things in our lives to occur, and we cannot change those things that we chose beforehand. I've prayed so many times for my eyesight to be clear, and this occurrence coincides with what happened to me. My eyesight was healed twice after I prayed for healing, but then returned back as it was. I now can remember *choosing* to have poor eyesight before my life on Earth.

***

Continuing with my vision:

After I chose my physical impairments for my life's journey, my male mentor, who was standing with me in front of this living book of my life, chose another physical impairment for me. To my recollection, I was to gain weight when I grew older and I remember agreeing and understanding how this would help me in my mission. The idea of gaining weight held no significant problem for me at all in Heaven. It really didn't seem to be a relevant issue to worry about any visual features of myself. Appearance on Earth had no value to the 'true' me in Heaven. While in Heaven, I didn't care what I looked like nor what impairment I had on Earth. I knew what I was supposed to accomplish in my earthly life, and that was the only thing that had any relevant value to me. I also knew that I would undergo a state of forgetfulness of my life in Heaven – a type of amnesia.

Next, I was asked to choose from a number of different categories, additional circumstances for me to learn, improve myself and help others. Within each category I was to personally select a choice from a list. The choices had a degree of value varying from slight to drastic, whereas the more drastic measures were worth much more toward my Heavenly destiny of winning a better, higher level closer toward God and with it comes many rewards, but the best reward was my closeness to God. I wanted to select one drastic challenge in at least one of the categories because I wanted the value and rewards of accomplishing the more difficult challenge. This makes sense to this verse: *"Others were tortured to death, disdaining release, to win a better resurrection."*[45] I didn't want to go through my life on Earth and not earn a new level. This would seem to be a waste of a valuable lifetime. I ultimately thrived on pleasing God. This brings me much joy! I desired to do anything that God wanted me to do and was joyfully anxious to accomplish His will, which directed my decisions.

---

45. Hebrews 11:35

I chose to grow through marital problems. This choice was very commonly used because it forces people to deal directly with disagreeable situations. It would be difficult to ignore and turn their backs away from facing problems when they had to live each day being personally involved. People who personally experience difficult situations must act upon them in one way or another. It's a stronger involvement than simply observing and learning from another person's problems from a distance.

My male mentor nodded and agreed with my choice, then he also added his choice to also be my marriage. "Oh, no," I thought. "I was given a double dose of marital problems!"

I wasn't given the details of the hardships, but I accepted with indifference that almost everyone deals with marital problems, so, I couldn't see what would be so difficult for me to deal with in my marriage. Knowing this was a double dose of marital hardship, I paused, took a deep breath, but understood that I had asked for something drastic to overcome.

The remaining categories could be slightly challenging, if I chose it to be so, in which most seemed to be a piece of cake, at least from my point of view in Heaven. My choices seemed to be nothing to worry myself over because I knew God's statutes in my heart and anything that's in my heart would stay through my life on Earth. If I could only concentrate on the stronger challenge, then I would attain my ultimate goal.

As I evaluated the value of each of the different options listed, I found that there was usually one option which caught my attention and I needed the remaining options on the list to fulfill my journey. It wasn't too difficult to decide which choice I wanted to be challenged by on Earth.

I was then told to choose a difficult hardship or problem that I could learn to overcome. I can't remember what I chose, but again my mentor always chose after me another level or degree of whatever we were asked to choose. My mentor chose something related to my family, like my first child. I couldn't understand how a child was a difficult situation to overcome, because I was thrilled to be given a child. But now, I am still living through a heartbreaking dilemma as my first child, now a young man, brings me understanding of how a child can bring emotional turmoil and a difficult, trying life. He rebelled against our parental warnings and chose to discover drugs and the harmful choices of a wayward youth.

***

I know the greatness of God's love for me, and I do not believe God is punishing me. Through these spiritual revelations, I now realize that this is one of the hardships that I needed to endure and learn to overcome. I am sieved through the trials of life only to become a greater jewel in God's eyes. It is through these difficult problems and heart-breaking ordeals that life pounds us into experienced beings - as gold is refined by the fire. I know that through my life lessons, God gave me the gifts of endurance, patience, and inner strength to see this through. In my trust in God, I know that some day my son will return as he began, for he had a good beginning. I have to continue to love him and hope forever. I handed him over to God, for I have learned that God will accomplish what seems to be the impossible in *His* time. This is yet another test of trust.

The trial of my son also has intertwined into a 'lesson door' for my husband. This has helped him to see himself a little better and became an opportunity to help him choose to work on improving himself. As painful as it is to see my son suffer, I am thankful that through the pain, there also comes healing. There is always hope. It's still a long process, but at least my husband is trying to understand how his aggression negatively impacts all of our lives. Now we wait for our son to choose a positive action.

So, now I see where a child can be a great difficult challenge. Life on Earth is not easy and it wasn't supposed to be. I only pray that I do what is correct in this mission. It is unsettling, to say the least, when I cannot help my son, no matter what I try. I am filled with frustration and disgust as he continues in his stubborn, unreasoning, and rebellious attitudes. My husband and I have had innumerable heart to heart discussions with our son, and we have told him that we love and care about him and wish him to be happy. Unfortunately, we cannot reach him yet. He built a barrier of great distance and disrespect, which we cannot penetrate. What is left for a parent to do but let their child reap what he deliberately chooses for himself. Why does he have this attraction to repel us and our help?

* * *

I can correlate my problem to God's dilemma in seeing His children go astray. I can see the similarity that perhaps the realm of Earth has many barriers which place a great distance between people and their love for God. I don't want to see my son go through the pain he is enduring and headed for in the future, but he was warned about the consequences, and still chooses this path. There must be a purpose in this, because I remember choosing to go through difficult trials for a purpose. Maybe it's to help me understand God's love for us; as a concerned loving parent cares for their reckless child headed for disaster. Maybe my problem is to help me to see through God's eyes the dilemma in trying to balance His love for us while permitting us to use our free will (which doesn't always lead us on the best path).

The human will is quite stubborn and sometimes unreasonable. No matter how God tries to guide us, most often we choose our will over His. Even though we were given many warnings that our ways lead to destruction, we rebel the warning. Now I understand why God watches from a distance. His heart is torn when He is closely involved. We don't listen to Him and so He lets us reap the consequences of our actions because we won't learn any other way. But from the distance, God has hope and enduring love for any who turn around to find His way. We have to want God's guidance to find it. It was there all along. We had a good beginning and I can't help thinking that God is waiting for our return with open arms, no matter how disastrous our choices were. We are like the prodigal son. I know that God's love endures forever. Even though I can't feel it in the Earth's realm, I felt it in the spirit realm. My love and hardship with my son is reflecting as a microcosm of God's heart.

It comforts me a little bit to know that this trial would have happened to me no matter what I did in the past because this was chosen as a spiritual lesson or trial. I am not a victim if I agreed to experience this lesson. I understand that I do not have control over stopping my son's choice if I want to honor his free will. If I imposed my authority over him, he felt pulled toward wanting to die because he had a strong will to choose differently than me. I don't want him to want to die, so I have to let go. I am supposed to learn from this and help him realize what he does – to accomplish an important lesson for all of us. I've learned that we cannot remove the free will of others. We may try to help others through example and through education, but each person's choices in their life is their own responsibility. Now that my son is an adult, I need to respect him and permit him to explore his choices for his life. I don't know the lessons that he signed up to learn for his growth and so I pray that he finds his way.

I could have chosen a life that wasn't too difficult, but I wouldn't accomplish much, and of course, I wouldn't receive many rewards, either. I wanted to advance to a new level in Heaven; what all that entails, I do not remember. I knew with *reason* why things happened on Earth while I was in Heaven, but now I have only faint remembrances. I know that to completely understand knowledge, we must have *experience* and first hand involvement. I now had to prove what I knew as correct, to attain my goal.

My children have helped me to understand many things about life that weren't possible any other way. Both of my children insisted that I help them with their algebra homework, except they wanted me to give them only the answers and closed their ears to my explanation of why or how to solve the equations. I would repeatedly explain that the numbers change and the operations may change, but if they would stop and evaluate why a certain problem is solved in a certain way, then they would be able to solve any future problems without constant assistance. I cannot be there with them while they take their tests at school. They must learn to solve problems on their own. But still, both of my children begged and whined for only the answers and detested listening to the explanation. I wondered whether they were too lazy or too impatient to learn the steps, but they must learn just as I did. People learn math by repetition and participation in homework. If they do not do the work for themselves, then they will not learn how to do things on their own.

This is why we are journeying through life lessons on Earth. The measure of knowledge is not just knowing the answers, but it is from the experiences of involvement that we can come to understand a solution. Our lessons would be so simple to solve if we had our memory from Heaven, but we're not looking for concluding answers, we're looking for reasons to understand *why* and *how*.

My family always wants me to do things for them. It is a battle to get them to do certain things for themselves. I do not wish to be their slave servant while they relax and do nothing that is their responsibility. I want to be a giving and sharing family, where each person is loved and appreciated instead of expecting all things done for them. Life is not to be one sided, where one is always the slave of the other. God does not want to be our slave either. He should not do all the work for us. We have to dig into our life lessons, even though we dread the repetition and hard work. We need to get out there and learn from life! Can you imagine all the questions and work each person asks of God? Multiply that by millions and billions of people. That's why God created the Earth school. God is awesome!

Eleven
Safety Bumpers

"we shall enter upon our heritage, when
God redeemed what is his own,
to his praise and glory"
Ephesians 1:14

Continuing further about my prebirth vision/memory:

The next set of choices surprised me. They were on the reciprocating side to balance the difficult lessons. I was told to choose a 'safety bumper' to help me from straying from my goal. I chose something, but I cannot recall what I chose, but then, my mentor also gave me a safety bumper. It had something to do with my husband. I was confused because I knew earlier that my husband was chosen to be a hard challenge to help me improve, learn and to help others. I didn't think to choose any of the choices I made under the hardship choices for an opposite reason. I glanced back at the previous choice of my husband listed under 'hardship' - *twice*, but didn't question the authority of my mentor. I thought it may be better for me that my husband would be both challenge and safety bumper, especially since he was a double challenge. Maybe the hardship half would ease up and wouldn't be as severe with the added influence of safety. I agreed with my mentor's choice. I was then directed to choose another extra precautionary bumper. I didn't think that I needed anything else since I already had two bumpers, but I chose again since I was directed to do so, and besides, what would it hurt? After choosing, I was confident that my heart would lead me through everything. I knew in Heaven with reason why things happen on Earth, although I did not consider fully what life on Earth would be like without my memory of Heaven.

I was then given another bumper which was my second child. This child was not to be a means to overcome a difficult lesson as my first child was. She was to help guard and coax me to stay on my path. I was extremely surprised and happy to be given another child to care for and raise. Being completely pleased, I thought two children were a blessing and a gift in my life.

Then came my last choice. This was my decision to choose the way I wanted to leave my earth life and return home. As I looked over the list, there were many options that had an uncertain amount of time feeling pain before leaving. There were also options without pain, but again the more difficult choices had more value and rewards. As I near the bottom of the higher-value choices, one option struck me as not seeming to be difficult for me. I chose this option to be my second difficult challenge, so I could earn more credit toward my goal just in case I didn't accomplish the first challenge.

***

I remember being enthusiastic about my coming to Earth for my mission and I knew that I couldn't fail because I had an understanding of what was right and what was wrong inside of me, and I would not forget or fail if I drew my knowledge from my heart.

***

Cleansed by the Spirit

Moving forward three months

On November 10, 2000, as I was walking through my bedroom, I felt something lightly touch the top of my head. I could not see it obviously, for I do not have eyes on top of my head, but I could feel it. As soon as I noticed it, I realized that it was as light as a feather. It began to descend down and into my head. It spread out as a flat disk of fire which reminded me of a wide laser beam. What was happening to me? I was caught off guard by this and didn't understand what this was. I stood quiet and still as it slowly penetrated down through my entire body. As soon as it reached my stomach, I felt nauseated to the point that I could hardly bear it. I reached out to the wall to hold myself up. The heat was so overwhelming that I sweat profusely, drenching my clothes in sweat. My clothes were so wet that I could probably wring water out of them.

The fire continued to descend all the way down to my toes. Once it reached the bottom of my feet, it immediately began to ascend back up through my body, all the way to the top of my head. I felt that I would fall down to the point of death as the sickness I felt was unbearable for about five minutes. Listlessly, I plopped down onto my bed like a rag doll. I had no energy to move as it knocked all energy out of me. While I lie upon my bed, I tried to figure out what happened to me.

After about five minutes passed, all of the sick feeling went away and I sat up in bed. I looked down at my clothes and noted they were completely drenched with sweat. A few minutes more passed and I discovered that my clothes had completely dried! How did the wetness dissipate and dry so quickly? The only description that I can describe how I felt at that moment, is that I felt purified. I felt washed and cleansed from the inside. I thought about this for a while and then realized that I was just baptized by the Holy Spirit with fire, just as it says will happen in the book of Acts!

I never really considered that this would actually happen to me. After all, I never knew of anyone else who had this happen to them. I looked up the story about Pentecost in the Bible[46] and read about the tongues of flame landing on the tops of the people's head, giving them power to speak in different languages. That's what landed on top of my head – a little flame! I did not receive a new language, but then I wasn't planning to be traveling in another country where I would need it. The scriptures say that there are many types of spiritual gifts. I wanted to know exactly what this meant. What was God trying to tell me? Was I given a

---

46. Acts 2:1-4 and 11:17

spiritual gift?

I contacted a few ministers and asked them if they had ever heard about anyone else ever receiving the fire of the Holy Spirit. Unfortunately, they had nothing to tell me beyond the story of Pentecost in the Bible. But why aren't there more people being baptized with the Holy Spirit, especially when Jesus told us about it?

Now that I have been led to write about my spiritual experiences, I can verify some of the scripture from the Bible because they came alive in my life. I became a witness to its truth. I finally know that I was accepted by God and given a mission to be a witness for God. The Bible says that the Holy Spirit *"is the pledge that we shall enter upon our heritage, when God redeemed what is his own, to his praise and glory."*[47]

The denial about any testimonies in regards to the presence of the Holy Spirit in our lives has been preventing people from finding God. Our testimonies are what has been missing from the

---

47. Ephesians 1:14

churches. Throughout all of these years ever since Christianity was controlled and manipulated by despotic leaders, they had literally shut the door in men's faces! Religion is supposed to inspire us and guide us to *find* God. It's not supposed to stifle the spirit of truth. I remember Jesus saying the same thing in his day when he criticized the lawyers and Pharisees.[48] This is still happening today! The despotic leaders of the church still try to silence people who actually find God and testify about it. Why? Don't they realize that they are trying to silence what Jesus encouraged us to discover? Who are they to denounce and control what the Holy Spirit does? Are they afraid to lose their unquestionable power and control over people? Are they afraid of being proven wrong? What if they are wrong! How does it help our world to perpetuate deception? What's more important here? Is it more important for people to actually turn to God for enlightenment or for people to follow religious leaders who don't truly understand the

---

48. Matthew 23:13

scriptures or the power of God? The scriptures are still valid that we may receive His Advocate - the Spirit of Truth - which teaches us all things, even about the nature of God.

This is how we may distinguish those who worship God in spirit and in truth from those who manipulate people to bow down to men. God does indeed teach us spiritual insights through divine revelations through the Holy Spirit. I feel so disgusted to find out how long so many of our religious leaders and despotic lawmakers have manipulated and controlled religion, preventing people from discovering their own connection with God. Here is the clogged artery! We must all turn back to God by contemplating about all things in solitude and sincerity. Don't let the blind lead the blind.

There is so much more to discover about God and spirituality if we will open up our hearts to embrace it. If we truly want to seek God then we need to expect and believe that He will send us the promised Holy Spirit to teach us the things of the spirit. We don't need men who had never experienced any spiritual experiences to teach us about it. They are blind guides because they do not understand what it's like. We need to seek the Glory of His Presence to come upon us so that we may be guided in spirit. I feel like shouting along with John the Baptist: "Open up your hearts and be baptized with the power of the Holy Spirit." Our Father God is waiting on us to welcome Him into our hearts. When we are ready, the Spirit will come! I testify that it happened to me and it can happen to you!

Twelve
A Shocking Epiphany

"When anyone is united to Christ, there is a new world; the old order has gone, and a new order has already begun."

2 Corinthians 5:17

As I thought about my prebirth visions and memories over the next several weeks and months, I would remember a little more detail each time. I remembered that a couple of assistants escorted me to another area to talk with someone else for more information. When we arrived, the assistants stayed behind as I casually walked beside a calm, gracious male guide as he tried to explain to me what it would be like to see darkness on Earth. I could feel his curiosity as to why I hadn't experienced darkness before, but he didn't ask me. He seemed a little shy, but very gentle as he just did what he was asked to do for me.

He said, "First of all, everything is half light and half darkness."

"Darkness!" I interrupted, "But, why is there darkness? Doesn't Satan rule in the darkness," I asked nervously as I wondered what I was getting myself into. He wanted to console my concern, "Yes . . . but this doesn't have anything to do with Satan . . . that's something different." He took a deep breath and then began, "God created the light and the dark, and the planets that orbit." (It seemed he was explaining Genesis with what I already knew, and I nodded my head in agreement.) I intercepted as we casually walked along and rattled on with my knowledge about creation.

Then I inserted, "But I never *experienced* life on Earth yet!" Although he didn't question me about this, I could feel that he thought this was unusual. Most of us have already experienced life on Earth. He walked me to a place where we stood on a platform of some sort. As I gazed out, I could see the planets up close and moving as though we were watching them from the universe. The planets were distinctly rotating and evolving in their orbits. I observed them up close and personal like an astronaut in outer space; except I was outside in the air. It was so vast and enormous!

Then he continued to explain the darkness, "Everything is black wherever you look. Even though things are still there, you can't see them because they look black and they blend into the blackness of the night around them . . . Here, shut your eyes." I closed my eyes and tried to visualize darkness with the color black. I thought about a black floor, black walls, and black furniture, but I could still see the pieces of furniture and the wall and floor. They did not blend together to where they were invisible to me in darkness.

I placed my hand over my eyes (just as he also began to cover my eyes with his hand, but since he saw that I placed my own hand over my own eyes, he put his hand back down.) My guide knew what I was seeing and said, "Almost . . ."

Then he searched for words to fully explain darkness, "Let me place my hand over your eyes, too." Then he placed his hand over my hand to make it seem darker, but I still vaguely visualized the surrounding and nothing seemed totally invisible. He said, "That's close, (as he somehow saw what I was thinking), but not quite. You'll see what I mean. Don't worry. It'll be all right." I knew some things were invisible in light, but I couldn't comprehend invisibleness in the dark.

***

That's where my memory ends of this event. I felt as though I was suddenly given part of my memory back from beyond. But how can I have a memory of all of this in my mind? I didn't do any of this in my life on Earth and I understood that it happened in another realm.

It is now January of 2001. I decided to share this vision/memory with Roy Mills, author of *The Soul's Remembrance*, since he also has memories from heaven. He made me feel comfortable to open up to what lie deep inside of me. I needed his contact because I felt so foreign in a world that denied what I *knew inside*. By now, we had only talked on the phone for about seven/eight months and never met in person yet.

As I told him about my vision, I was knocked off my feet when Roy intercepted my story when I got to the part about the two assistants escorting me to chat with another guide.

Roy said; "This sounds familiar. I have the very same memory."

He was drawing from his own mind a similar heavenly memory, only he said it from his own perspective that was very similar to mine. Then he told me what happened next before I told him! How could he know what happened in my vision? What's going on here?

He continued to share with me his memory as we continued chatting on the phone. He just jumped right in and said that I was concerned about the darkness and Satan, and that I was worried about Satan ruling the darkness. What! How could he know that! I hadn't told him that part yet, for I hadn't remembered until he mentioned it. He verified things I hadn't said yet and also brought to mind what I forgot. He said that he was amazed with the wisdom that I had as he listened to me talk about creation. I felt shocked! This vision/memory that I had was real! This memory is from before I was born and Roy was this guide! It was then that we realized that we were connected to each other with the same incident in Heaven. Talk about a jolt in my mind! His memory of his incident *was* my incident!

Roy and I had never physically met each other on the Earth at that time, but he verified some things about the incident without my telling him. I know that he told the truth for how could he had known what I tried to visualize in heaven while he described this incident over the phone? How could he know the details that I hadn't told him yet? Wait, maybe he was reading my mind over the telephone. That's possible, . . . but, then am I reading his mind because I also knew what he felt in this memory before he told me? How could I have known what was in his thoughts in that realm before he mentioned it over the phone? He said several things that verify what I saw. How could he know that? Then, how could I do the same about him? I wasn't reading his mind because I had this vision before we talked on the phone. Oh, my goodness! I don't understand how this can be!

I could not remember from my vision/memory what my guide's face looked like, but I could feel that it was Roy by comparing the way he talks with the way the guide talked. They were so similar that I could almost visualize his face and body in my mind, but not clearly. I felt puzzled that I could remember so many details and yet the faces were blurred. I was ecstatic to find someone who confirmed and remembered an event that I had in Heaven! This really verified that my vision/memory happened long before I was born. We were both alive in Heaven before being born on Earth! But can my conscience accept this without going mad? I was aghast! Oh God! I've always wanted to find the truth but I wasn't quite ready for this! This is quite a stretch for me.

I understand how some people have difficulty believing in angels and apparitions, but the things of the spirit are unfathomable to our minds. As I contemplated about this memory, I thought; "Isn't it ironic that people understand how tangible colored objects can look invisible in the dark of night, but cannot understand the same in the light. God created the light and the dark, and everything visible and invisible."

We talked the following day and verified even more detail and other memories. We had connected to a mission that we were both involved with to help humankind. Then I continued to tell Roy that I remembered a small room where a group of us gathered to discuss all of our plans and missions together. We were finalizing the missions of our future life that each of us participated in choosing. We had our individual assignments for Earth, and yet we were all connected somehow in another expanded mission. We were all going through the same process individually and as a group with interlinking soul agreements.

I was sitting in the front row of seats, while a male, whom may have been Roy (it feels to me that it was him), was over to my right side. (My memory is partial, without seeing faces.) We were all instructed to face forward as we watched someone with greater authority address us. He had greater authority because he gave permission to one of us for something without asking a higher authority, and he directed our meeting. He was the overseer of our soul group. We had a lot of freedom but at the same time we always had to ask permission for anything different from the norm because each of us wanted all of our missions, individually and as a group, to succeed. We were working in cooperation with one another.

We discussed our individual missions, the abilities each of us were given, and events that would happen. When it came to my turn for the higher authority to summarize my life mission with the group and zoned in on my life events and abilities, our group began to worry about something about our connected mission. (I can't remember the details of what we discussed.) Just then, the male beside me, who felt to be Roy, stood up and faced us. "Don't worry, I've been given permission to remember everything," he soothed. I started to feel a smidgen jealous that I was not given the gift of full memory, but then I was contented knowing that I was given partial memory at the right time. I knew it would be enough to help me accomplish my mission and with his memory to help all of us remember, everything would fall into place. I did not become envious of Roy, but understood that each of us were given just what we needed and the abilities suited for our purpose. Our lives intertwined and then separated. We had common goals and individual goals.

That was the end of my memory of this event. Roy listened intently as I recalled this memory, and felt that it may have happened, but he couldn't recall it just yet.

Days later, Roy phoned me back. He was

excited as he exclaimed, "I know what we were worried about! We were afraid that our personal lives and problems would keep us so busy and we were all so far apart on Earth that we were afraid we wouldn't remember our mission when the time was right." When Roy explained that to me, I knew that he hit the nail on the head! He worded it *exactly* as the concern was expressed in this memory and I knew that was the reason that he stood up beside me in Heaven and explained to us that he was granted permission to remember.

He continued explaining further memories that he had from Heaven. Amazingly, Roy told me about two of the people that were there with us in that soul group and he already had contact with them on Earth. This is amazing and unbelievable! He encouraged me to contact them and gave me their phone numbers. (They had come forward to contact him because they also remembered things from Heaven. The first woman, Kay, went to one of Roy's lectures and recognized him immediately from Heaven. The second woman, Tam, read his book and recognized his picture in the back of the book.)

This was the first time that I had ever thought about people coming *to* Earth *from* Heaven. I thought that we only go *to* Heaven after we die. This is all turning around. Also, I thought that we began life at conception. I now know that only the physical body begins at conception. Our spiritual body was already alive, just not enclosed within a frame, or vessel as I call it. In Heaven, we are who we are now, except not confined in physical skin. You can't see the spiritual body in this world, unless God permits it. We may have spiritual beings all around us and never know it. *"The dust returns to the earth as it began and the spirit returns to God who gave it."*[49] The things of the spirit just keep shocking me!

This was all so unbelievable and bizarre! I needed some time to swallow what I had just discovered. This was a much larger chunk than I was ready to swallow. I was curious but quite

---

49. Ecclesiastes 12:7 and 3:21

nervous to contact the two women whom Roy referred to me. After waiting a few weeks, I decided to call Tam. She was very friendly with a bubbly personality. I liked her right away and we talked for a long time about spiritual matters. She had such a clear memory of Heaven that was more miraculous than my memory. I then told her about the small room where a group of us met. She then agreed that we were discussing our missions but she couldn't remember this with many details. I told her that my memory of Heaven was triggered when I read the book, *Plato: The Last Days of Socrates*.

Tam told me that her memory of Heaven was triggered as soon as she had recently finished reading the Bible from cover to cover. I was excited to hear that she was also writing a book about her memories of Heaven, although she hadn't published it yet. She shared her spiritual experiences with me and we also discovered several linking spiritual incidents, just like Roy and I had. Boy, the Bible isn't kidding when it says: *things beyond our seeing, hearing, and imagining!* I felt speechless with awe! We were coming together with a similar mission, just as in the vision that Roy and I remembered worrying about. Is this what the scriptures mean about our desire to have our mortal body absorbed into the life immortal?[50] And also: *"When anyone is united to Christ, there is a new world; the old order has gone, and a new order has already begun."* [51]

"[May the Lord] give you help from the sanctuary and send you support from Zion!"[52] I wonder if the place we are remembering is the same place the scripture is referring to as Zion?

It surely seems as though my vision/memory was bringing a lot of scripture to life. Even though I had evidence that these spiritual visions were real, I had a hard time accepting it, yet how could I deny it? I asked myself: "Do I want to stay in ignorance as the world thinks and believes, or do I want to

---

50. 2 Corinthians 5:4-5

51. 2 Corinthians 5:17

52. Psalm 20:2

reach into the *real* truth!" I asked for the truth, so I'd better prepare myself for what I get.

If I can only digest this, then I consider myself in good company with many wonderful people, including Jesus and his disciples, and all the people of God. They were all so brave to step into the light of the Truth even when the world rejected and persecuted them. I understand their concern and I don't want to let them down by not coming forward with my testimony. If the world still chooses to lash out against me as well for speaking about spiritual truth, then I'll just have to go down that road. There's no turning back now. I know my ultimate destiny will be at rest in the presence of God. Jesus said, *"In very truth I tell you, he who receives any messenger of mine receives me; receiving me, he receives the One who sent me."*[53]

It was almost beyond my grasp and too good to be true, and yet I had evidence in the scriptures which came true in my life and also in my prebirth memories which correlates with other people's

---

53. John 13:20

prebirth memories.   I wanted to call the other woman that Roy encouraged me to contact, but something inside me wanted to wait for a while. I needed to swallow and digest this new concept before I went any further. I wasn't quite ready to take another bite. On the other hand, I was anxious to find out if Kay remembers me and anything else about our mission.

As far as I can remember now, my mission was to write this book and the unfinished information from Socrates. He wasn't able to share it in his day but it is still needed today to help people understand what they do and why God sent us to Earth. If I want to make a difference in this world, then I must continue to seek the truth and prepare myself for new revelations.

It is difficult to find out that so much of what so many religious leaders teach isn't even close to the real thing. It's just the watered down version that's only the tip of the iceberg. The scriptures are still valid, and many ministers do try to teach the message of love and light, but our churches are also mixed with deceptions that have nothing to do with spiritual truth. It is hard to grasp spiritual truth because it goes far beyond what the clergy taught. These insights have really helped me to see where religion has gone astray and built up walls of deception to keep us from finding God. If their ways are correct, then how is it that I have personally found God and they have not?

I wonder what may be ahead of me now? There must be more to my mission than just my book, for why would all three of us remember being together in Heaven for a united mission if there wasn't something monumental to do for God? I realize that some things I've written are eye-poppers for some people to swallow, but I don't think anything was too monumental, considering God's power and purposes. I'm sort of bracing myself for the next miracle. Even Jesus said, *"I send you therefore prophets, sages, and teachers."*[54] *"'And they shall all be taught by God,' Everyone who has listened to the Father and*

---

54. Matthew 23:34

learned from Him comes to me."[55]

Now I know what Jesus meant when he said, *"If anyone wishes to be a follower of mine, he must leave self behind; he must take up his cross and come with me. Whoever cares for his own safety is lost; but if a man will let himself be lost for my sake, he will find his true self.*"[56]

Everyone who listens and learns the ways of God will ultimately transform their lives through the spirit until they find this secret treasure, for Christ came to show us the way through the veil of darkness. We are the body of Christ, working together to carry out God's mission. Each of us must try our best to reach our highest potential so that we may also help others to reconnect homeward bound.

So, now I have found evidence that I was alive before I was born on Earth! Do the scriptures testify to this? *"The word of the Lord came to me [Jeremiah], '**Before** I formed you in the womb I*

---

55. John 6:45

56. Matthew 16:24-26

*knew you for my own, and **before** you were born I consecrated you.'"*[57] The words are all there, it's just that my mind couldn't conceive of this reality before or that it could be referring to me too. Jeremiah was a child when the 'word of the Lord' told him that God knew him before he was in the womb.

And then the verse; *"he who has come from God has seen the Father."*[58] I saw the Father during my near-death-like experience. Then, this scripture is verifying what I just discovered through the spirit; that I came from God. I was hidden in this world and I did have a purpose! Now I understand why I was sent back to Earth after my NDLE. I needed to get to work on my mission that I had forgotten until now.

This is all so astonishing to me, and I'm the one who experienced it! I decided to stand up against the false ideologies and give testimony to my story. Just as the reoccurring dream I used to

---

57. Jeremiah 1:4-5
58. John 6:46

have as a child of being chased by the demon, it's all intimidation because no person has any power over my soul. I must forego my fears of the world's critics and tell the truth. Faith is dead if we don't act on it.

Talking with Roy about this event verifies that we volunteered for a special mission. All of us remember leaving Heaven to come to Earth with a mission. *"They are <u>strangers in the world</u>, as I am. Consecrate them by the truth, thy word is truth. As thou hast sent me into the world, <u>I have sent them into the world</u>, and for their sake I now consecrate myself, that they too may be consecrated by the truth."*[59]

Each of us are testifying about our prebirth memories of coming from the realm of Light to help humankind embrace our on-going existence. There are millions of people all over the world who have had spiritually transformative experiences besides us, who are also encouraging and inspiring people to discover their spiritual identity. We are all

_____

59. John 17:16

pitching in to uncover this truth and this book is my attempt to do my part.

The scriptures make even more sense to me now! I had touched and experienced what they are talking about in the spirit! *"[I pray that God] may give you the spiritual powers of wisdom and* **vision***, by which there comes the knowledge of him. I pray that your* **inward eyes** *may be illumined, so that you may know what is the hope to which he calls you, what the wealth and glory of the share he offers you among his people in their heritage, and how vast the resources of his power open to us who trust in him. They are measured by his strength and the might which he exerted in Christ when he raised him from the dead, when he enthroned him at his right hand in the Heavenly realms, far above all government and authority, all power and dominion, and any title of sovereignty that can be named, not only in this age but in the age to come. He put everything in subjection beneath his feet, and appointed* <u>him</u> *as supreme head to the church, which is his body and as such holds within it the* *fullness of him who himself receives the entire fullness of God."*[60]

All praise be to God! I couldn't have learned any of this without the help of my Advocate, the Holy Spirit. *"It is time to act, O Lord; for men have broken thy law. Truly I love thy commandments more than the finest gold. It is by thy precepts that I find the right way; I hate the paths of falsehood. Thy instruction is wonderful; therefore I gladly keep it."*[61]

This is why Jesus forewarned us that the Father will send the Advocate to teach us everything.[62] It's about time to see this fulfilled.

***

As I ponder about the choices that I made in Heaven while I took part in collaborating my life lessons before being born, and compare them with

---

60. Ephesians 1:17-23

61. Psalm 119:126-129

62. John 14:26 and Acts 2:39

my actual life, I can see the connection. In Heaven, my marriage was chosen to be a double dose of hardship as well as a safety bumper. Even though our marriage went through many difficulties and drained me to my lowest point of depression, I was determined to stay through the trials. These trials were the means that taught me about life on earth and the difficulties were individually designed for me to learn difficult lessons. Without them, I would not have been driven to seek God's help with so much determination. God did not forsake me. I was renewed through spirit with a sense of purpose.

Who would have known that by reading *Plato: The Last Days of Socrates*, a book that my husband bought for me to read, would be the key to unlocking my prebirth memories!

I have grown in understanding spiritual things that was needed to bring me closer to what I had forgotten prior to earth life. By writing these chapters, I was brought to see the correlation of my life lessons and my actual life. All of the people in my life have taught me so much that I couldn't have learned any other way. Life is very hard for everyone but we must persevere through our struggles to win the race of a grander life. All of us have learned from one another and I am truly grateful for all that people have done to help me grow.

I have learned so much through scripture as they came alive within my life. I understand why the scripture says, *"that our mortal part may be absorbed into life immortal."*[63] When I returned back into my body after my NDLE in 1984, I felt my body absorb my spirit like a sponge and through my prebirth memories, I discovered that my soul is immortal. Perhaps this is what Jesus meant when he said that we need to be born again of spirit. I don't think that I would ever come to understand the things of the spirit if I hadn't had my NDLE and other spiritually transformative experiences. They were all essential in transforming my mind and heart in embracing a deeper understanding of spirituality.

---

63. 2 Corinthians 5:5

I now know that I existed before my life on earth and that my life was somehow planned out, at least to some extent. Even though some events were pre-planned, the unfolding of my life on earth was affected by the choices that I made here.

It is so very difficult to live on earth now that I remember about my previous life in Heaven because I want to go back. I understand what Jesus was talking about when he said; *"I know where I come from, and where I am going."*[64] Jesus was sent by the Father and he said that we shall do as he has done. It never occurred to me that I would discover that I was also sent for a mission to witness for others! It's difficult for me to acknowledge this and yet I cannot deny my memories. No church that I know has ever come close to explaining this to their congregation. That's probably why I feel so torn about this discovery. Even though I know what I experienced in the spirit is true, my mind still struggles to completely embrace it because it goes against what so many of us were taught. I'm still

---

64. John 8:14

working on this and I'm a work in progress.

I hope that my experiences will be helpful. I live each day in anticipation for God to reveal Himself to me again. I'm still learning about the spirit but I know that there is no death of my soul. I will continue to wait as long as I must and do whatever it takes to go back home to God. I hope that I will fulfill my commitments and finish my mission because that's why I came.

My soul was planted into this body. That's why Jesus uses parables about gardens, farming, and harvest. The earth really is not our home. Our true home is in Heaven and this is why Jesus said that he belongs to the world above.[65] Most people are afraid of dying only because they do not understand or remember what it is like in Heaven. *"Whenever he turns to the Lord the veil is removed. . . and because for us there is no veil over the face, we all reflect as in a mirror the splendour of the Lord; thus we are transfigured into his likeness, from splendour to splendour; such is the influence*

---

65. John 8:23

of the Lord who is Spirit."[66]

It has taken me 39 years before I found a tiny entrance in my veil where I could remember my true source. Jesus crossed through the veil as forerunner so that we will be comforted when we find that we are able to follow through the veil as well. I also discovered some of the things that he taught about the spirit which verifies and supports my experiences. It is these that God reveals to us through the Spirit; things beyond our seeing, things beyond our hearing, and things beyond our imagining![67]

***

I partially remember other things that happened in Heaven, but they are still cloudy and tiny glimpses of memory. I know that when the time is right, I will be given more memory. Some things that I remember would still be difficult for the world to accept even now in the 21st century! This world is

---

66. 2 Corinthians 3:15-18

67. 1 Corinthians 2:10

not so advanced in the truth as we want to believe we are. We seem to be stuck in the back ages about our spirituality and haven't gone forward. I'm willing to tell anything God wills me to say when He wants it told. I am anxious to do His work, but I must show my patience to wait on God to do His will, in His time, for His purpose.

***

After I finished reading <u>The Last Days of Socrates</u> at age 39, I began writing about the insights that I connected to from Heaven. As I wrote, thoughts flowed freely through my hands as though I was being led to write. In my next book I will share these insights that I discovered through spiritual vision. While in Heaven I wanted to inform people about life, death, and God by using the concept of positive and negative to encourage people to continue with further contemplation. It is my sincere hope and wishes that our world today will understand and take advantage of the wisdom contained in these divinely given insights. I can see how the evolution of humanity will evolve further along towards a higher destiny if we will open our hearts to recognize and embrace our divine nature and live it.

Bibliography and Additional Reading

Bainton, Roland. *Horizon History of Christianity, The*. New York: Harper and Row, 1964.

Charles, R.H. *The Book of Enoch*. Oregon: Wipf and Stock Publishers, 2002.

"Christianity." *Funk and Wagnalls Standard Reference Encyclopedia*, Volume 6. New York: Standard Reference Works Publishing Company, Inc., 1959 ed..

"Constantine." *Funk and Wagnalls Standard Reference Encyclopedia,* Volume 7. New York: Standard Reference Works Publishing Company, Inc., 1959 ed.

Cox-Chapman, Mally. *The Case for Heaven, Messages of Hope from People who Touched Eternity*. New York: The Berkley Publishing Group, 1995.

Eadie, Betty. *Embraced by the Light*. California: Gold Leaf Press, 1992.

From Jesus to Christ. PBS and WGHB/
   FRONTLINE,1998.
   <http://www.pbs.org/wgbh/pages/frontline/s
   hows/religion/why/legitimization.html>.

Gough, Michael. *The Early Christians, Ancient
   Peoples and Places*, Series Vol. 19.
   Frederick A. Praeger, Inc., 1961.

Hamilton, Edith. *Witness to the Truth.* New York:
   W. W. Norton, 1957.

Hebrew Greek Key Word Study Bible, NIV.
   Tennessee: AMG International, Inc., 1996.

Marchiano, Bruce. *In The Footsteps of Jesus.*
   Harvest House Publishers, Oregon and
   Visual Entertainment, Texas, 1997.

Mills, Roy. *The Soul's Remembrance.*
   Washington: Onjinjinkta Publishing, 1999.

New English Bible with the Apocrypha, The. New
   York: Cambridge University Press, 1961,
   1970.

Plato, The Last Days of Socrates. Translated by
   Hugh Tredennick and Harold Tarrant.
   England: Penguin Books Ltd., 1993.

Robinson, James (General Editor). *Nag Hammadi Library in English, The.* Revised edition. New York: HarperCollins Publishers, 1990.

Scholem, Gershom. *Kabbalah.* Jerusalem: Keter Publishing House Jerusalem Ltd., 1974.

The Gospel According to Matthew (The Visual Bible). VHS Tape. Tennessee: Visual International, 1994.

The Lost Books of the Bible and The Forgotten Books of Eden. World Bible Publishers, Inc. (The Lost Books of the Bible. Alpha House, Inc., 1926 and The Forgotten Books of Eden. Alpha House, Inc., 1927.)

Vermes, Geza. *Complete Dead Sea Scrolls in English, The.* New York: Penguin Putnam Inc., 1998.

Wilson, Ian. *Jesus: The Evidence.* New York: Harper and Row Publishers, Inc., 1984.

Wilson, Ian. *Jesus: The Evidence.* Washington, DC: Regnery Publishing, Inc., 2000.

Glossary of Terms

ADC (After-Death Communication) - paranormal phenomena which includes a communication with an entity or spirit which was once a living person.

Awakenings - a transformation about who you are in connection with the spirit realm.

Enlightenment, sacred, mystical or religious experience - caused by divine agency rather than ordinary natural processes. They are real encounters or real contact with higher-order realities of which humans are not ordinarily aware.

Kundalini - an indwelling spiritual energy that can be awakened in order to purify the body system and ultimately to bestow the state of divine union upon the seeker of truth.

NDE (Near-Death Experience) - a spiritual, transcendental or other-worldly event that can occur during a clinical, imminent or possibly imminent death situation. The NDE can also occur while suffering from trauma or while having an intense desire to die.

NDLE (Near-Death-Like Experience) - same general elements and aftereffects as an NDE, but were not in any health crisis or near clinical death.

OBE (Out of Body Experience) - A perception of life from an outside position of the physical body.

Pre-birth memories - having memories of a life existence before being born

Past-life experiences - recalling a life lived from a previous life experience, as another person.

Revelations - information received through a type of spiritually transformative experience.

Spiritual Emergencies - where an individual experiences sudden, drastic changes to their meaning system (i.e., beliefs, identity, purposes, goals, values, etc.)

Spiritually Transformative Experiences (STEs) - Any type of experience that has an etherial or spiritual awareness which affects one's prior state.

Visions - a supernatural experience that conveys a visual perception or sight seen from the frontal lobe.

Websites and Contact Information to Organizations Devoted to Types of Spiritual Experiences

After-Death Communications - http://www.after-death.com/   PO Box 916070, Longwood, FL 32791

After Death communication Research Foundation (ADCRF) - http://www.adcrf.org/ PO Box 20238, Houma, LA 70360

American Center for the Integration of Spiritually Transformative Experiences (ACISTE) - www.aciste.org   PO Box 1472, Alpine, CA 91903-1472

Eternea - http://www.eternea.org/   PO Box 871, Deerfield Beach, FL 33443-0871

International Association for Near-Death Studies (IANDS) - http://iands.org/home.html 2741 Campus Walk Avenue, Building 500, Durham, NC 27705-8878

Institute of Noetic Sciences (IONS) - http://www.noetic.org/   625 2nd St., Suite 200, Petaluma, CA 94952-5120

The Monroe Institute - https://www.monroeinstitute.org/   365 Roberts Mountain Road, Faber, VA 22938

NDE Space - Near Death Experience Network - http://www.ndespace.net/

Near Death Experience Research Foundation (NDERF) http://www.nderf.org/   and Out-of-Body Experience Research Foundation (OBERF) http://www.oberf.org/ - PO Box 20238, Houma, LA 70360

Near-Death Experiences and the Afterlife - http://www.near-death.com/

New Heaven New Earth (NHNE) - http://the-formula.org/

Nour Foundation - http://www.nourfoundation.com/   322 West 108th Street, New York, NY 10025

Omega - http://www.eomega.org/   150 Lake Drive, Rhinebeck, NY 12572

The Rhine Research Center - http://www.rhine.org/   2741 Campus Walk Avenue, Building 500, Durham, NC 27705

Society for Psychical Research - http://www.spr.ac.uk/main/

CPSIA information can be obtained
at www.ICGtesting.com
Printed in the USA
LVOW03s1428210817
545792LV00019B/882/P